The "I Don't Know How to Cook" Book

MEXICAN

300 EVERYDAY EASY MEXICAN RECIPES—
THAT ANYONE CAN MAKE AT HOME!

LINDA RODRIGUEZ

adamsmedia
Avon, Massachusetts

Published by Adams Media, an F+W Publications
Company
57 Littlefield Street
Avon, MA 02322
www.adamsmedia.com

ISBN 13: 978-1-59869-607-3
ISBN 10: 1-59869-607-6

Library of Congress Cataloging-in-Publication Data
is available from the publisher.

Printed in the United States of America.

J I H G F E D C B A

This publication is designed to provide accurate and
authoritative information with regard to the subject matter covered. It is sold with the understanding that the
publisher is not engaged in rendering legal, accounting, or
other professional advice. If legal advice or other expert
assistance is required, the services of a competent professional person should be sought.
    —From a *Declaration of Principles* jointly adopted by a
        Committee of the American Bar Association and
            a Committee of Publishers and Associations

Contains material adapted and abridged from *The Every-
thing® Mexican Cookbook* by Margaret Kaeter, copyright ©
2004 by F+W Publications, Inc.

This book is available at quantity discounts for bulk purchases.
For information, please call 1-800-289-0963.

Contents

Acknowledgments

Mary-Lane Kamberg wrote the first *"I Don't Know How to Cook" Book*, a simple and simply brilliant concept. I'd like to thank her for beginning this series. Special thanks to my husband, Ben Furnish, and my children, Crystal, Niles, and Joseph. And above all to the late Jenny Rodriguez, who taught me how to cook Mexican so long ago.

I would particularly like to thank my friends, Ruben and Norma Campos, who own my favorite Mexican restaurant, Chelly's Café. They have been generous with their time and answers to my questions. My gratitude goes also to the Latino Writers Collective for encouragement, support, and general crazy fun.

Thanks, too, to my editor, Chelsea King, who made this process so painless.

Introduction

The original concept of *The "I Don't Know How to Cook"
Book* was to create a hands-on learning experience for
new cooks. In *The "I Don't Know How to Cook" Book: Mexican,* I have a similar goal—to make Mexican cooking so
easy and so much fun that even inexperienced cooks
can enjoy a successful south-of-the-border cooking
adventure in their own kitchens.

If you love Mexican food as much as I do, you're in
for a delicious treat. You can make it yourself by following the easy directions you will find here. There are
no fancy cooking terms in the recipes, though you can
find them in a glossary at the end of the book for use
with more traditional cookbooks. Also, I have taken
advantage of the wide variety of already prepped and
cooked foods available to the modern cook to make
the cooking process quicker and simpler. Your greatest
difficulty may be in finding specific Mexican foods and
seasonings, but in recent years most of the specialty
items required in these recipes have become widely
available throughout the United States.

Some of the dishes most identified as Mexican in
the United States are actually Tex-Mex, a style of cooking that developed out of the centuries-long interac-
tion between U.S. settlers in the Southwest and the
Mexicans and Indians they found already living there
and influencing each other's language, dress, art—and
food. We've included these dishes, such as fajitas, in
this cookbook, too.

The recipes in this cookbook are grouped according to difficulty within each chapter and identified by these symbols:

LEVEL **E**

SERVINGS **4**

Easy: **E**
Medium: **M**
Hard: **H**

Vegetarian recipes are identified with a "**V**" right after the recipe title; vegetarian recipes do include eggs. Serving size is indicated below each "easy" level.

Although some of these recipes are classified as "hard," they are not really difficult, but they may require extra steps or a slightly more advanced technique. Begin with the many recipes marked "easy" and "medium." Then try one of those marked "hard," and you'll be pleasantly surprised at how your cooking skills have developed.

It won't be long until you're planning a fiesta with your friends, and this is very authentic since Mexican and Mexican American cooks love to cook for their family and friends. Just practice your recipes for yourself first. Before you know it, you too will be always ready to pull up another chair and get out another bowl or spoon.

Chapter 1

Get to Know Mexican Foods

If fast food tacos and burritos are your idea of Mexican food, you're in for a surprise. No one eating what passes for commercial Mexican food in America would have any idea of the variety of tastes and textures good Mexican food provides—or the variety of fruits and vegetables (almost always missing on that restaurant plate) found in good Mexican cooking.

Myths and Misconceptions

Unfortunately, overeager restaurateurs striving to bring Mexican cuisine into our lives perpetuate some common misconceptions about Mexican food. In their efforts to create meals that appeal to a palate not accustomed to spicy foods, they have eliminated the subtle blending of flavors and the wonderful textures in Mexican meals. Even many of the more authentic Mexican restaurants tend to provide only the menu items that are familiar to most Americans—enchiladas, burritos, tacos, and tostados, and always with sides of beans and rice.

Blend, Blend, Blend

Mexican cuisine has actually changed very little over the several thousand years that the country has been settled. Europeans brought new varieties of meats, vegetables, and cheeses, but the basic tenets of Mexican cooking are the same today as in the days of sun goddesses and tall pyramids.

Mexicans blend everything. There is absolutely no mixture of foods and spices they won't try. To the Mexican cook, separate flavors are good, but when they are combined, they create something so unusual, so mouthwateringly wonderful, that you just have to try adding another combination of ingredients. Marinate the steak in garlic and olive oil? Sure, but can't we add just a little oregano, a few peppers, and some green tomatoes?

At first, the tastes might seem too different, but you will quickly come to appreciate the melded flavor as something new in and of itself. Don't worry that you find pork or poultry mixed with papayas and peppers. It's Mexican. Don't fret when you find chocolate in your meat sauce or wine in your eggs. It's Mexican. And don't cringe when you see specks of chili powder in your candy or peanuts and fruits floating in your water. The blend of flavors is tantalizingly, uniquely Mexican.

As a result, you will quickly find that Mexican cooking uses just a few basic main ingredients—meat, beans, rice, tortillas, fruits, and vegetables—but combines them in a multitude of different ways:

Soups: These may be blended together, or they can be European style with larger chunks of meat.

Dry Soups: These are more like casseroles. They start with a soup consistency but use rice, tortillas, or bread to soak up the ingredients.

Stews: These are exactly like their European counterparts, mixing large chunks of meats, fruits, and vegetables.

Moles: These thick, heavy sauces can be used as toppings for whole pieces of meat such as chicken breasts or they can be cooked with chunks of meat to use as stuffing for tamales.

Salsas: Salsa literally means "sauce" and can be used to describe anything from a watery salad dressing to a thick mixture of tomatoes, onions, and spices.

Common Spanish Cooking Terms

We're going to steer clear of traditional cooking terms in this cookbook, but I will use some authentic Mexican terms for food or preparations. That way, when you set an authentic dish before your friends, you'll be able to use its real name. Here's a list of definitions to keep in mind as you cook:

Verde: green, usually meaning the recipe uses green tomatoes or tomatillos

Picadillo: shredded meat, vegetable, and/or fruit filling

Salsa: sauce

Relleno: stuffed

Arroz: rice

Pollo: chicken

Nopale: cactus paddle

Carne: meat, usually beef

Raja: roasted chili strip

Lomo: pork

You can also refer to the glossary (see Appendix B) for more listings.

Tortillas

Of course, the more you blend your ingredients, the more you need something to put them in. Enter the tortilla. Be it rolled, folded, fried, baked, or soaked, it's still a tortilla.

History of the Tortilla

The corn tortilla is distinctly associated with Mexico. The ancient people of Mexico made tortillas by letting the corn kernels dry on the ears in the fields. The kernels were soaked in lime water until the skins could be rubbed off. The wet corn then was ground on a flat stone until it was a fine powder that could be used to make dough. The dough was made into thin patties, then baked over open fires.

Today, true Mexican food aficionados will still make their tortillas this way. However, the Mexican homemaker is more likely to buy masa harina, dehydrated masa flour. Although some people try to substitute cornmeal, that doesn't work well. Masa harina is actually made from white corn, as opposed to the yellow corn more popular in the northern climates, and it has a much finer texture than cornmeal. You will find it in most large supermarkets today.

In northern Mexico and the Southwest, tortillas made with wheat flour have been common since the early nineteenth century. These traditional flour tortillas are quite large and so thin as to be translucent, but few people have the time or talent to make them like that any longer so they are not commonly found elsewhere. However, the modern flour tortilla, smaller and a little too thick to see through, has made its way everywhere that Mexican cooking can be found.

Healthy Tortillas

Health-conscious people also have altered the traditional Mexican tortilla. Some people add ingredients such as tomatoes, spinach, or spices to the masa flour to create a healthier or more flavorful tortilla.

As with any culture's cuisine, Mexican food is always changing. Most Mexican cooks now use flour tortillas for some dishes and some are experimenting by adding spices or other flavors. Relax. If you like sun-dried tomato tortillas, it's okay. You will still be eating authentic Mexican cuisine. You won't be eating it in the style of ancient civilizations, but you will be eating it in the tradition of change and adaptation that the people of Mexico have used to create the wonderful cuisine that is theirs today.

Chili Peppers

After the tortilla, probably the one food most often associated with Mexican cooking is the hot chili pepper. Unfortunately, most people assume this means that the dish must be hot, when the opposite is often true. The chili peppers are added for flavor and sometimes for spice, but even a large dish will often contain only a couple of chili peppers, along with a similar amount of onion.

In ancient times, the chilies were added partly to help preserve food but also to add unique tastes to the ubiquitous turkey meat they ate. For centuries, the meat eaten by almost all Mexicans was turkey. Beef, chicken, and pork came only with the Spaniards. As a result, one common cooking technique is to change the type of chili peppers added to a sauce. By doing this, you can create a completely different dish.

It's not hard to do. There are nearly seventy varieties of chilies, ranging in size from that of a large pea to nearly a foot long. They come in many colors, ranging from red and purple to green and yellow. As a general rule, color has no effect on flavor, but size does: the smaller the chili, the hotter it tends to be.

If you don't like the spice chili peppers add to your foods, don't leave them out completely. Just add fewer. Or, instead of chopping the pepper into small pieces, add it whole and remove it before serving the meal. That will provide some of the flavor without adding any unwelcome bits to the dish.

Seven Chilies You Need to Know

1. *Jalapeños:* These chilies are almost universal. Either red or green, they reach about three inches and have a medium heat.

2. *Poblanos:* These are dark green, medium-sized peppers that are often used for roasting or stuffing. They are relatively mild, only slightly hotter than sweet bell peppers. When dried, they are called ancho chilies and used for several classic sauces.

3. *Chilies de arbol:* These dried red chilies are long and thin with a papery skin. They are very hot.

4. *Chipotles:* These are dried or smoked red jalapeños. They are usually dark reddish brown and add a smoky flavor to dishes. They are milder than fresh jalapeños but still have a bite.

5. *Moritas:* These are dried, smoked jalapeños. They are small and brown with a spicy taste. They are not as smoky as chipotles but are hotter.

6. *Habaneros:* This is the hottest of the chilies. They are lantern-shaped and can be orange, red, or green.

7. *Serranos:* These are small, thin chilies that taste similar to jalapeños but are a little hotter. The red ones are a little sweeter than the green.

Spices

Mexican cooking uses a number of spices that are unique to the cuisine. However, it's more usual to see a combination of more common spices working together with chili peppers to create the unique Mexican flavor. There is very little that you can't find in a well-stocked grocery store. And, if you really want to try a dish that calls for something unique, it's likely you can find it at a specialty store such as a food co-op, Mexican grocery, or import grocery. Many of these offer mail order or have Internet presences, also. Or you can do as Mexican and Mexican American cooks have done for centuries when living in a part of the United States that had no access to their traditional foodstuffs—improvise with the foods you can find.

Mexicans take their flavorings seriously. Many recipes call for you to roast the spices first. Some will have you using only fresh herbs because the dried variety will either lose their flavor or create a totally different flavor.

Following are seasonings you should know how to obtain before you start any Mexican recipe:

Anise: This is used in many dishes. The leaves, which can be difficult to find, are used to wrap food in, but dried, ground anise is used to flavor anything from candy to stews.

Annatto seeds: Also called achiote, these are the seeds from a tropical tree. They have a musky, earthy flavor. Achiote is used as a commercial dye to add orange tints to cheeses and other foodstuffs.

Chili powder: There are as many different types of chili powder as there are chilies. Most are simply dried, ground versions of chili peppers although some contain mixtures of different chili peppers. It's best to experiment to find your favorite, and I have also included an easy recipe for making your own chili powder. Note that chili powder is usually added for its flavor, not to make the dish taste hotter.

Cilantro: Also known as coriander when we use its seeds, the fresh herb has a unique, strong flavor. This is one of the herbs that must be used in fresh form, but fortunately in recent years it has become common in American grocery stores, since it is a necessity for Asian cooking as well as Mexican. It can usually be found in the produce sections next to the fresh parsley.

Cinnamon: For best results, look for the rough-edged variety from Sri Lanka as opposed to the tightly wound variety used in the United States, but the U.S. variety will work if you can't find the other.

Cloves: These are often used as part of a spice mixture for moles and sauces. They are most commonly used in ground form, although traditionally whole cloves are among the many different spices ground together with nuts, chocolate, and chilies to make moles.

Cocoa: This is not sweetened. The sweetened variety is never used, not even semisweet chocolate. Traditionally, Mexicans used ground cocoa beans. A good dark cocoa is your best bet to emulate that fresh-ground Mexican cocoa.

Corn husks: Dried corn husks are most often used to make tamales. They are first soaked in water. They are actually considered a spice because the flavor is transferred to the corn flour when steamed. This is why traditional cooks will line the bottom and sides of their tamale steamers with corn husks—to increase that subtle flavoring.

Cumin: This lends a distinctly Mexican flavor to many dishes. It's usually used in ground form, although you can buy the whole seeds and grind them if you want the freshest flavor possible.

Epazote: This herb's strong, bitter flavor can dominate any dish, and for this reason, it is the one herb most often used alone in Mexican cooking. It actually is treated as a weed in North America but can still be hard to find in a grocery store. Although the fresh has the best flavor if you can find it, you can use dried, which is stocked in most Mexican grocery stores.

Nutmeg: This is often used as part of many spice mixtures.

Oregano: More than a dozen different varieties grow in Mexico and it's the most common herb in the Mexican kitchen. You will only need dried, as Mexican cooks almost always use this herb in its dried form, even when they have it growing in a little plot outside their kitchen door.

Tamarind: This is a tough brown seed-pod that produces a sticky paste. It is the main ingredient in Worcestershire sauce but makes a refreshing popular cold drink.

Nuts

Nuts are used as both a spice and a thickening agent in many Mexican dishes. Among the most common you will find in Mexican recipes are:

Cashews: use unsalted, fresh-roasted when possible.

Peanuts: skinless, unsalted are the best, if available.

Pepitas: a pumpkin seed.

Pistachios: a wrinkly green nut. (Do not use the white or red dyed types.)

Beans

In ancient times, when the only source of meat protein came from turkeys, Mexicans turned to beans for both variety and to provide other proteins. As a result, the bean was a staple of the Mexican diet long before the Spanish arrived, and they continue to be popular today.

Most of us associate either black beans or the pinkish pinto beans with Mexican cooking. However, there are more than twenty different varieties of beans that are commonly used in Mexican dishes. A Mexican kitchen has as many different types of beans as the Italian kitchen has pasta shapes.

There is no one right bean for any recipe. In the countryside, the Mexican cook will have her own garden and plant the varieties her family likes. In the city, people will buy what they like or what the grocery store has in stock that day.

However, the various beans do taste different, so it's worth experimenting. The milky lima bean, for example, will give a totally different flavor to a refried bean dish than the heartier black bean. In the end, though, if you like it, that's all that counts.

No one really knows why the Mexicans started creating Refried Beans. Perhaps it was a way to make a quick dish out of their staple food. They could prepare the beans days and even weeks beforehand, then just recook them as needed.

The easy way to make your Refried Beans is from canned beans, but I have also included easy recipes to cook your own pinto and black beans so you will also be able to make your Refried Beans fresh, if you prefer. Resist the urge to serve them right out of the pot though. Letting them sit in the refrigerator for a day or two before mashing them with spices and reheating them lets the true flavor of the beans emerge.

Cheese

Cheese didn't exist in Mexico until the Spanish conquistadors brought milk animals to the land. In nearly 500 years, though, Mexican cooks have embraced both the flavor and nutrition in cheese by adding it to many of their dishes. They also have developed some of their own unique cheeses that have yet to be exported from the country in large amounts.

However, most Mexican cheeses either have a similar European counterpart or they don't play a crucial role in the dish. As a result, many Mexican cooks will substitute a common European cheese from time to time. Also remember that Mexican cooking is known for being able to adapt to the ingredients available. If you can't find an authentic cheese, don't be concerned. A transplanted Mexican cook just uses what's available!

Cheese Substitutes

Following are some of the common cheeses used in Mexican recipes along with their European substitutes. Note that in this book we did the work for you and listed the substitute.

Queso añejo: This means "aged cheese." Parmesan and Romano are good substitutes.

Queso de bola, quesillo de Oaxaca, and asadero: These are made by cooking the curds and pulling them into long strings. Although they have a unique flavor, mozzarella is a good substitute.

Queso Chihuahua and queso menonita: These are hard, aged cheeses that have a mild flavor. Mild or medium-sharp Cheddar is a good substitute. Colby also works well.

Queso fresco: This means "fresh cheese." Fresh ricotta or a mild fresh goat cheese is a good substitute. Cottage cheese also works well.

Queso manchego: This is a semisoft cheese that melts easily. Monterey jack is a good substitute.

Queso panela: This is a semisoft cheese that looks like mozzarella but does not melt well. Cottage cheese and ricotta are good substitutes.

Meats

Poultry, red meat, fish, and seafood are important ingredients in Mexican cooking, but they more often are on the receiving end of the spicy sauces. As a result, they don't get a great deal of attention in most Mexican recipes. In fact, a typical recipe will call for "carne," or simply beef. Even when making seafood meals, the authentic recipes usually don't specify what main ingredient to use.

Still, there are things to keep in mind. Mexico is a large exporter of beef, so it is readily available in Mexico. However, many people don't have refrigerators, and beef is still relatively expensive. As a result, it is often reserved for special meals.

Pork is more common than beef in daily meals but lamb is actually the most common red meat. Poultry is still the protein of choice for most Mexicans.

For people who live on the coasts, seafood is a common meal. Interestingly, it has as many variations as the red and white meats in terms of sauces and mixtures, but fish is actually grilled more often than meat. It's common to serve a grilled lobster tail with absolutely no sauce, while beef or pork is never served "naked."

It's important to know your fish when using it in cooked meals, especially the moles or picadillos. You need a fish that will keep its consistency, not turn rubbery, or, worse yet, disintegrate into the mix. Most recipes do well with bass or flounder. If you have a wide variety of fish available in your area, it's best to ask the fish seller how the fish holds up to long cooking before you try it.

Vegetables and Fruits

With a subtropical climate, there are no shortages of fresh vegetables and fruits in the Mexican diet. Perhaps the only truly unique item in this arena is cactus. Mexicans put nopales, or cactus paddles, in a number of different recipes, treating it almost as those in the United States treat string beans or broccoli. Nopales aren't difficult to cook, but, unless you live in the Southwest, it can be very difficult to find fresh ones.

Today, it's very easy to find fresh tropical fruits in even the northern-most grocery stores. It can take a little bit of time to learn how to peel or deseed these fruits, but it can be well worth the effort to gain a taste of the real thing. Canned fruits virtually never taste the same as the fresh variety.

Putting It All Together
Mexicans like to eat. In fact, they eat more meals than most of the rest of the world. If you're putting together a true Mexican feast, it might be fun to devote an entire day to the Mexican style of eating. Here's what you would do:

Desayuno is served early in the morning and usually consists of coffee with milk and tortillas.

Almuerzo is served mid-morning and includes eggs, beans, tortillas, chili sauce, and coffee.

Comida is served mid-afternoon during the siesta period, when the sun is at its peak. Many businesses close so people can go home for this meal. It begins with appetizers and is followed by soup. The next course is a dry soup followed by fish or meat with a salad and vegetables. The dessert is a sweet or fruit.

Merienda is served in the early evening. It is usually a cup of hot chocolate or coffee with tortillas.

Cena, or supper, is served any time after 8 p.m. If comida was a large meal, this will be a light meal. How-ever, if it is a fiesta, the meal will start as late as midnight and rarely before 10 p.m. In this case it might be served more as a buffet or, in the case of a formal gathering, it will have even more courses than the comida.

Don't let all this background information fool you, though. This book is full of "easy" recipes. Those marked "medium" usually just have a few more steps in them, and the "hard" ones aren't really difficult at all. So even if you're new to cooking, you can put together authentic Mexican meals right from the beginning. Let's get started now!

Common Measurements
These common measurements will help you in this cookbook and any other!

3 teaspoons = 1 tablespoon

4 tablespoons = ¼ cup

5 tablespoons plus 1 teaspoon = 1/3 cup

1 cup = ½ pint

2 cups = 1 pint

2 pints = 1 quart

2 quarts = ½ gallon

4 quarts = 1 gallon

Chapter 2
Appetizers and Salsas

This basic recipe can be altered to your taste by adding more and different chilies, or by adding beans and vegetables.

Also, try adding fresh or frozen corn.

Use a pair of kitchen shears to cut up the canned tomatoes and chilies while still in their cans.

?

Tomato Salsa v

What You Need

1 medium yellow onion

1 (4-ounce) can green chilies

1 (14½ ounce) can diced tomatoes

¼ cup fresh cilantro

What You Do

1. Remove skin from onion and cut into ¼" pieces.

2. Cut chilies and tomatoes into ¼" pieces.

3. Chop cilantro into ¼" pieces.

4. Combine all ingredients and let sit overnight in a covered container in the refrigerator.

Tortilla or Tostada?

Although many North Americans associate crispy corn tortillas with tacos, tostadas are the only item that calls for frying the tortillas until it is crisp and hard. Mexicans rarely use the formed, fried tortillas we see at Mexican restaurants. Instead, they heat the soft corn tortilla, place the meat in the middle, and fold it over.

This is excellent served with tacos or as a dip for tostada chips.

Green Tomato Salsa   v

What You Need

1 large white onion

1 (11-ounce) can tomatillos (also sometimes called "green tomatoes"), with liquid

1 bunch fresh cilantro

¼ cup canned sliced jalapeño peppers

2 teaspoons salt

1 teaspoon ground black pepper

What You Do

1. Remove skin from onion and cut into ¼" pieces.

2. Put tomatillos (with liquid) in food processor or blender. Blend on medium setting for 30 seconds.

3. Roughly chop cilantro so pieces are about ½" long.

4. Combine all ingredients. Mix well.

5. Refrigerate for at least 12 hours before using.

Are Green Tomatoes Edible?

Although we tend to think of green tomatoes as unripe, and therefore not fit to eat, the opposite is true. Because they have a firmer flesh and more tart taste, they add a distinctly different flavor from their ripe counterparts. Eating green tomatoes also means we get to enjoy the fresh garden tomatoes for a longer season.

This is the perfect dip for tortilla chips.

It also makes an excellent sauce to pour over enchiladas.

Chili con Queso v

What You Need

1 medium yellow onion

5 dried chipotle peppers

2 medium tomatoes

¼ cup canned sliced jalapeño peppers

2 tablespoons vegetable oil

½ teaspoon garlic paste

1 (8-ounce) package shredded Monterey jack cheese

1 (8-ounce) package shredded Colby cheese

1 cup sour cream

What You Do

1. Remove skin from onion and cut into ¼" pieces.

2. Break off stems and empty out seeds from chipotle peppers and chop into ¼" pieces.

3. Cut tomatoes and jalapeños into ¼" pieces with kitchen shears.

4. Heat oil at medium temperature in a large skillet. Add onion. Cook until tender but not brown. Add garlic, chipotle peppers, jalapeño peppers, and tomatoes. Cook for 3 minutes, stirring constantly. Turn heat to medium-low. Add cheeses to pan and cook, stirring constantly, until cheese melts. Stir in sour cream.

What Kind of Cheeses are Used in Mexican Cuisine?

Like virtually every culture in the world, the various regions of Mexico have their own types of cheese. Unfortunately, few of these are available outside of Mexico, even in authentic Mexican restaurants. At the same time, because Mexican cuisine was influenced by Spanish cuisine centuries ago, the world of European cheeses is used in their recipes.

For a less spicy sauce, keep the jalapeño whole and remove it after simmering the mixture.

Basic Picante Sauce v

What You Need

1 large white onion

¼ cup canned jalapeños or 1 whole jalapeño pepper

2 (14½-ounce) cans diced tomatoes, drained

3 tablespoons vegetable oil

1 teaspoon salt

¼ teaspoon sugar

1 tablespoon fresh, chopped cilantro

What You Do

1. Remove skin from the onion and chop into ¼" pieces.

2. Cut jalapeños and tomatoes into ¼" pieces with kitchen shears while still in can or measuring cup.

3. Put oil in a large frying pan and preheat to medium temperature. Add the onions and cook until tender and golden but not brown.

4. Add remaining ingredients. Turn heat to medium-low and simmer about 10 minutes.

?

Is Mexican Water Really Impure?

Mexicans know the importance of drinking lots of water in their hot climate. So why don't they get sick? The truth is that they do get sick when they go to other parts of the world. Every region has different bacteria in the water that its inhabitants quickly grow immune to. The water that gives us "Montezuma's Revenge" is not impure, it is simply the local variety.

This is a wonderful topping for potatoes and meat dishes as well as a popular dip for tortilla chips and raw vegetables.

Guacamole v

What You Need

2 large, ripe avocados

1 medium red tomato

1 small yellow onion

½ cup canned jalapeño peppers

1 tablespoon lime juice

1 teaspoon salt

½ teaspoon ground black pepper

What You Do

1. Cut avocados in half lengthwise and pry out pits. Peel and cut the avocados into 1" pieces. Mash with a fork.

2. Cut tomato into ½" pieces. Remove skin from onion and cut into ¼" pieces. Drain water from jalapeño peppers and cut into ¼" pieces.

3. Combine all ingredients. Mix well.

This is the classic enchilada or burrito sauce.

It also can be made with other chilies.

Red Chili Sauce   v

What You Need

12 dried red ancho chilies

1 small white onion

3 large red tomatoes

4 cups water

½ teaspoon garlic paste

¼ teaspoon salt

What You Do

1. Break off stems and shake out seeds from ancho chilies.

2. Peel onion and chop into ¼" pieces. Chop tomatoes into ¼" pieces.

3. Place all ingredients in food processor or blender (in several small batches) and purée.

4. Put the sauce in a medium frying pan on medium heat. Cook for 30–40 minutes, until sauce is smooth.

How Do I Choose the Right Pan for Cooking?

When choosing a pan for cooking on a stovetop, make sure the food comes no closer than two inches from the top of the pan when all ingredients are added. If the food fills the pan more than that it won't cook evenly.

Green Chili Sauce   v

Use as a green sauce for tacos, enchiladas, or any other dish.

What You Need

1 cup fresh green chilies, your choice

1 cup canned tomatillos with juice

¼ cup fresh parsley

¼ cup onion

1 garlic clove

¼ cup canned jalapeño peppers

1 teaspoon salt

½ teaspoon ground black pepper

¼ cup olive oil

What You Do

1. Remove peel, stems, and seeds from green chilies.

2. Put green chilies, tomatillos with their juice, parsley, onion, clove, jalapeño peppers, salt, and black pepper in a blender or food processor. Blend to a purée.

3. Heat oil in a medium frying pan to medium heat. Add sauce and cook about 5 minutes, stirring constantly.

Can Cayenne Pepper Be Used in Making Chocolate?

We often overlook cayenne pepper as a spice but it does some interesting things, especially when added to chocolate. It loses most of its flavor while retaining the heat. And, most interesting, it literally heats up a person's body. It was the secret ingredient of the chocolatier in the movie *Chocolat.*

While salsas are always delicious with tortilla chips, try something different and serve dollops of salsa on toasted French bread or use garlic bagel chips for dipping.

Roasted Red Pepper Salsa ⌄

What You Need

2 large red bell peppers

¼ cup olive oil

12 green onions

1 can sliced black olives

⅓ cup Parmesan cheese

4 tablespoons lime juice

3 tablespoons fresh cilantro

½ teaspoon salt

½ teaspoon ground black pepper

What You Do

1. Remove core and seeds from red peppers. Slice into ½"-wide strips. Coat insides with olive oil and bake at 350°F for 1 hour or until lightly brown. Let cool, then chop into ¼" pieces.

2. Remove skin from green onions and discard all but 2" of the white and green part. Chop into ¼" pieces.

3. Combine all ingredients in a medium-sized mixing bowl. Cover and refrigerate for 12 hours. Let stand until mixture reaches room temperature before serving.

Serve with
Grilled Swordfish
(see page 164).

Pineapple & Mango Salsa   v

What You Need

½ cup fresh mango

½ cup cucumber

1 medium tomato

½ cup fresh or canned pineapple chunks with juice

3 tablespoons green onions

⅓ cup chopped red bell pepper

3 tablespoons fresh cilantro

1 fresh jalapeño pepper

½ teaspoon salt

What You Do

1. Remove skin and seeds from mango. Cut fruit into ½" pieces. Peel cucumber and cut into ½" pieces. Cut tomato into ½" pieces. Reserve juice from pineapple, mango, cucumber, and tomato.

2. Remove roots and cut green onions into ½" pieces. Remove stem and seeds from red bell pepper and cut into ½" pieces. Remove stems and cut cilantro into ½" pieces. Remove stem from jalapeño pepper and cut into ½" pieces.

3. Combine all ingredients, including juices and salt. Mix well. Refrigerate at least 4 hours before serving.

What are Tomatillos?

Tomatillos are an essential ingredient in many Mexican dishes. They are pale green or yellow and encased in a papery husk which is removed before cooking. Avoid any with shriveled husks. The canned variety are easy to find. Don't hesitate to substitute these for green tomatoes in any recipe, although they are slightly more tart than tomatoes.

This is a wonderful salsa served with chicken or veal because its light flavors don't overpower the meat.

Cucumber & Lime Salsa v

What You Need

2 medium cucumbers

2 Key limes

1 medium white onion

2 sprigs parsley

¼ cup lime juice

1 teaspoon salt

1 teaspoon sugar

½ teaspoon ground black pepper

½ teaspoon garlic powder

What You Do

1. Peel cucumbers and cut into ½" cubes. Peel Key limes and cut into ½" squares. Peel onion and cut into ¼" pieces. Chop parsley into ¼" pieces.

2. Combine all ingredients in a medium mixing bowl. Cover and refrigerate 3–4 hours before using.

This makes an excellent sauce for chicken but also works well as a dessert when put into warm Flour Tortillas (see page 286).

Dried Fruit Salsa v

What You Need

¼ cup golden raisins

¼ cup dried apples

¼ cup prunes

¼ cup dried apricots

¼ cup dried pears

¼ cup dried peaches

¼ cup pecans

1 small green onion

1 cup dry white wine

What You Do

1. Cut all dried fruits into ¼" pieces. Chop pecans into ¼" pieces. Peel green onion and remove roots. Chop onion and stem into ¼" pieces.

2. Combine all ingredients in a mixing bowl. Mix well so wine covers everything.

3. Cover and refrigerate 8–10 hours before serving.

Use this as a unique enchilada or taco sauce.

It also makes an excellent marinade for pork chops.

Chipotle Salsa v

What You Need

6 dried chipotle peppers

½ cup water

1 medium yellow onion

3 medium red tomatoes

2 tablespoons olive oil

1 teaspoon garlic paste

½ teaspoon oregano

½ teaspoon salt

½ teaspoon pepper

½ teaspoon sugar

1 tablespoon lime juice

What You Do

1. Break off stems from chipotles and shake out seeds. Place in a small saucepan with ½ cup water. Turn temperature to low and simmer for 15 minutes or until peppers are puffy. Drain water and chop peppers into ¼" pieces.

2. Peel onion and chop into ¼" pieces. Cut tomatoes into ¼" pieces.

3. Heat olive oil in a medium frying pan at medium heat. Add onion, garlic, and chili peppers. Cook until the onion is clear and limp, not brown. Drain excess olive oil.

4. Add tomatoes, oregano, salt, pepper, and sugar to frying pan. Stir well. Cover and simmer on low heat for 20 minutes.

5. Remove from heat and cool. Stir in lime juice. Refrigerate at least 4 hours before serving.

Pumpkin Seed Salsa

This sauce can be used like this for dipping; or, by adding two more cups of chicken broth, you can use it as a sauce when baking chicken.

What You Need

1 heaping cup pepitas (hulled pumpkin seeds)

1 small white onion

½ cup fresh cilantro leaves

2 large radish leaves

3 small romaine lettuce leaves

3 serrano chilies

1½ cups chicken broth (see Chicken Stock, page 124)

½ teaspoon garlic paste

1 tablespoon olive oil

What You Do

1. Place the pumpkin seeds in a large skillet over medium heat. Spread out the pumpkin seeds and toast, stirring regularly, until nearly all have popped and turned golden. Spread on a plate to cool.

2. Peel onion and cut into quarters. Remove stems from cilantro, radish, and romaine leaves. Tear lettuce leaves into pieces. Remove stem and seeds from serrano chilies and cut into pieces.

3. Put all ingredients in blender or food processor. Blend on medium setting until you have a smooth purée.

4. Pour olive oil into frying pan. Add purée. Cook on medium setting, stirring, until the sauce is thick.

How Do I Roast Nuts?

Roasting nuts must be done slowly or else the nuts will taste bitter. After you have roasted any nuts, pick out those that have dark brown or even black places. If roasting them to eat, add a tablespoon of sugar to each cup of nuts to make your own pralines.

Pear Ginger Salsa v

Use as a sauce for chicken or other poultry dishes.

It also makes a unique dip for Tostadas (see page 287).

What You Need

1½ cups canned pears

½ cup red bell pepper

2 scallions

1 tablespoon canned jalapeño pepper

⅓ cup golden raisins

1 tablespoon white wine vinegar

2 teaspoons fresh grated gingerroot

1 teaspoon salt

What You Do

1. Drain juice from pears and cut into ¼" pieces. Remove stem and seeds from red bell pepper and cut into ¼" pieces. Remove peel, root, and stem from scallions and mince. Drain juice from jalapeño pepper and chop fine.

2. Combine all ingredients in a medium mixing bowl.

3. Cover and refrigerate 8–12 hours.

Rooster's Bill (Pico de Gallo) v

You will find this different from the *pico de gallo* that your favorite Mexican restaurant serves, which is made from diced tomatoes, onions, and peppers.

Use this as a sauce for tacos or as a side dish for a meal such as Mexican Meat Loaf (see page 108).

What You Need

1 medium jicama

1 small yellow onion

1 large orange

1 tablespoon lemon juice

1 teaspoon salt

1 teaspoon chili powder

½ teaspoon ground oregano

What You Do

1. Wash, pare, and chop jicama into ½" chunks. Remove skin from onion and cut into ¼" pieces.

2. Pare and section orange, reserving juice, and add to jicama. Pour orange juice over mixture. Add onion, lemon juice, and salt. Stir until evenly mixed.

3. Cover and refrigerate at least 1 hour before serving. Sprinkle with chili powder and oregano before serving.

How Did *Rooster's Bill* Get Its Name?

This recipe got its name because it is frequently served by street vendors as finger food for their standup diners. The action of eating with the fingers is compared to the rooster pecking at corn in the farmyard.

LEVEL **E**

SERVINGS **6**

Heat and serve over anything from pork chops to cheese-stuffed jalapeño peppers.

Nogada Sauce v

What You Need

1 cup walnuts

½ teaspoon garlic paste

5 peppercorns

¼ cup bread crumbs

2 tablespoons cider vinegar

2 tablespoons sugar

½ teaspoon salt

6 tablespoons water

What You Do

1. Add walnuts, garlic, peppercorns, and bread crumbs to a food processor or blender. Blend until finely ground.

2. Add mixture to vinegar. Stir well. Stir in sugar and salt. Add just enough water to make a thick sauce.

For a change of taste, substitute orange juice for the lemon and lime juices.

Citrus Salsa   v

What You Need

2 large ripe tomatoes

1 medium white onion

1 fresh jalapeño pepper

¼ teaspoon fresh cilantro

¼ cup lime juice

1 teaspoon lemon juice

1 tablespoon dry cooking wine

1 teaspoon chili powder

¼ teaspoon garlic powder

½ teaspoon ground black pepper

What You Do

1. Cut tomatoes into ¼" pieces. Remove skin from onion and chop into ¼" pieces. Remove stem and seeds from pepper and cut into ¼" pieces. Chop cilantro into ⅛" pieces.

2. Combine all ingredients in a medium mixing bowl. Stir until well mixed.

3. Cover and refrigerate overnight. Let stand at room temperature 1 hour before serving.

How Do I Use a Blender?

Blenders can be messy business. Cover the top of the blender with a dish towel while using. Never fill a blender more than halfway. Always have about half liquid in the blender to offset the solids. Always leave a crack open at the top. Start blending by "pulsing" a few times to make sure the blades are running freely.

This is typically served over meat.

If making a pork or beef dish, reserve some of the stock and replace the chicken stock with that.

Adobo Sauce

What You Need

6 dried ancho chilies

1 large white onion

½ teaspoon garlic paste

1 cup canned tomatoes

½ teaspoon oregano

½ teaspoon cumin

2 tablespoons vegetable oil

1½ cups chicken stock (see Chicken Stock, page 124)

1 teaspoon salt

½ teaspoon ground black pepper

What You Do

1. Remove stems from chilies and chop chilies into ¼" pieces. Peel onion and chop into ¼" pieces. Drain tomatoes.

2. Add chilies, onion, garlic, tomatoes, oregano, and cumin in a blender or food processor. Blend to a thick purée.

3. Heat oil in a medium skillet to medium heat. Add purée and cook about 5 minutes. Stir in chicken stock, salt, and pepper.

Brie & Papaya Quesadillas v

Serve as an
appetizer with
guacamole, sour
cream, and Pico de
Gallo (see page 26).

Or add some
spicy chicken to
the quesadillas to
create an easy, one-
dish meal.

What You Need

½ medium yellow onion

½ cup water

1 pound Brie

2 large red jalapeño peppers

1 ripe papaya

4 tablespoons butter

12 flour tortillas (see Flour Tortillas, page 286)

4 tablespoons oil

What You Do

1. Remove peel from onion and cut into ¼"-thick slices. Heat the water in a medium skillet over high heat until boiling. Remove from heat and add the onions. Let stand 10–15 minutes. Drain and set aside.

2. Cut brie into ¼" strips. Remove stems and seeds from jalapeño peppers and dice into pieces about ⅛" square. Peel papaya and remove seeds. Dice papaya into pieces about ⅛" square.

3. Melt butter in a small saucepan over low heat. Add the oil to the butter and stir until mixed. Preheat oven to 250°F.

4. Place strips of cheese on half the tortillas. Add onion slices, ¼ teaspoon of diced peppers, and 1 tablespoon of diced papaya. Add another tortilla to make a sand-wich. Brush the top tortilla with the butter and oil mixture. Place the quesadillas one at a time in a skil-let on medium heat. Brown on buttered side, then flip and brown the other side. Keep quesadillas warm on a cookie sheet in the oven as others are being made.

5. Cut quesadillas into 6 triangular wedges to serve.

If you can't find plantains, try this same technique with bananas.

Use bananas that are just starting to ripen so they hold up better to the cooking process.

Fried Plantains v

What You Need

12 plantains

¼ cup vegetable oil

½ teaspoon salt

¼ cup ground horseradish

¼ cup sour cream

¼ cup brown sugar

¼ cup honey

What You Do

1. Remove skins from plantains and cut into 2" lengths. Using a heavy spatula, press down on each piece, round end up, until it is ¼" to ½" thick. They should be about the size of a fifty-cent piece.

2. Pour oil into a medium-sized skillet and turn to medium heat. Fry plantain patties until they are lightly brown on each side.

3. Make one sauce by combining the horseradish, salt, and sour cream. Make another sauce by combining the brown sugar and honey. Use the sauces for dipping the hot plantain patties.

Serve with broken,
warm Tostados for
dipping.

Spinach con Queso v

What You Need

1 (10-ounce) package frozen, chopped spinach

1 small white onion

1 medium red tomato

½ cup whole milk

1 (2-ounce) jar diced pimientos

1 pound Velveeta with jalapeños

What You Do

1. Thaw spinach and squeeze water from it until spinach is as dry as possible.

2. Remove skin from onion and chop into ¼" pieces. Chop tomato into ¼" pieces.

3. Combine milk, onion, pimientos, cheese with jalapeños, and tomato in a medium pot over low heat (or in a slow cooker set on the lowest temperature setting). Cook, stirring periodically, until cheese melts. Stir in spinach.

Serve with an assortment of fresh salsas for an interesting treat.

Mexican Roll-Ups v

What You Need

½ cup pitted black olives

2 fresh jalapeño peppers

1 bunch green onions

2 (8-ounce) packages cream cheese

½ teaspoon garlic salt

½ teaspoon chili powder

6 flour tortillas (see Flour Tortillas, page 286)

What You Do

1. Chop olives into ¼" pieces. Remove stems and seeds from jalapeño peppers and chop into ¼" pieces. Remove roots from green onions and chop onion and stems into ¼" pieces.

2. Combine all ingredients and mix until blended.

3. Spread on tortillas. Roll up.

How are Green Onions and Scallions Different?

Scallions are small yellowish onions that have a relatively mild flavor. Green onions are elongated white onions that grow no bigger than your index finger. It's common to eat the stems of green onions as you would chives.

These can be made ahead of time and frozen.

They can be reheated in a microwave.

Tomato Empanadas   v

What You Need

½ pound butter

1 (8-ounce) package cream cheese

2 cups flour

2 medium red tomatoes

1 small yellow onion

What You Do

1. Mix butter and cream cheese until creamy. Add flour and mix well.

2. Roll into a ball, cover and chill at least 4 hours,

3. Preheat oven to 350°F.

4. Cut tomato into ¼" pieces. Peel onion and cut into ¼" pieces. Mix tomato and onion together.

5. Roll out dough to about ¼" thick. Cut into circles about 3" across.

6. Put 1 teaspoon of tomato and onion mixture in the center of each circle. Fold in half and seal edges with a fork. Prick top of each one with a fork.

7. Place on cookie sheet and bake 15–20 minutes.

?

How Should I Choose an Appetizer?

Appetizers should complement the meal to come, not overpower it. Serve items that have milder but similar flavors to the main dish. Remember not to have so many appetizers that the guests aren't hungry for the main meal.

LEVEL **E**

SERVINGS **8**

Serve this with broken fresh Basic Corn Tortillas (see page 285).

Queso Fundido v

What You Need

½ pound Cheddar cheese, shredded

½ pound Monterey jack cheese, shredded

3 medium eggs

½ cup Green Tomato Salsa (see page 13)

What You Do

1. Preheat oven to 350°F.

2. Mix cheeses together and place into a large baking dish.

3. Beat together eggs and Green Tomato Salsa. Pour over the cheeses.

4. Bake for 30 minutes.

?

When Should I Grease the Pan?

Some recipes ask you to grease a pan before baking the ingredients. Others don't. The reason is that dishes with a fair amount of fat in them, such as that in cheeses, will create their own layer of grease on the bottom. Those that are primarily flour or have a lot of lean vegetables will have a tendency to stick to the baking dish if it isn't greased.

Totopos

Change the ingredients to suit your whims.

Hot peppers, beef, and guacamole also make good toppings.

What You Need

1 small yellow onion

1 cup shredded lettuce

1 fresh red tomato

2 cups Spicy Chicken (see page 125)

1 tablespoon butter

2 cups canned kidney beans

1 teaspoon salt

½ teaspoon ground black pepper

2 tablespoons white wine vinegar

1½ teaspoons sugar

¼ teaspoon garlic salt

⅓ cup vegetable oil

12 Tostadas (see page 287)

¾ cup crumbled goat cheese

What You Do

1. Peel onion and chop finely. Shred lettuce. Remove stem from tomato and cut into ¼" slices. Warm chicken in a small pan on low heat.

2. Melt butter in a medium frying pan on medium heat. Add onion and cook until limp but not brown. Add kidney beans with their liquid and salt and pepper. Cook until liquid is reduced by half.

3. Mix white wine vinegar, sugar, garlic salt, and ⅓ cup vegetable oil in a small covered container. Shake until well mixed. Combine lettuce and chicken in a medium bowl. Mix with wine vinegar and oil dressing.

4. Spread beans ½" thick on tostadas. Pile salad mixture on top. Add tomato slices and sprinkle with cheese.

What's the Meaning of *Totopos*?

Totopos literally means toppers. It's also the word used for the condiments served with tacos or when serving "make your own" tostadas.

Mexican Popcorn

While not as common a treat in Mexico as in the United States, popcorn is a common crop and it is frequently served at parties.

What You Need

1 pound bacon

½ cup butter

1 teaspoon chili powder

¼ teaspoon garlic salt

¼ teaspoon onion salt

½ teaspoon paprika

4 quarts popped popcorn

1 cup canned French-fried onions

What You Do

1. Preheat oven to 250°F.

2. Cook bacon in a large frying pan until very crisp. Drain grease and cool bacon on paper towels. When cool, crumble bacon into small pieces.

3. Melt butter in a small saucepan. Add chili powder, garlic salt, onion salt, and paprika. Stir until well blended.

4. Pour butter mixture over popcorn and toss until well covered.

5. Add bacon and onions to popcorn and toss lightly.

6. Pour mixture onto a cookie sheet and place in oven. Bake for 10 minutes.

Serve with freshly fried and salted Basic Corn Tortillas (see page 285).

Layered Mexican Dip v

What You Need

3 medium ripe avocados

2 tablespoons lemon juice

1 teaspoon salt

1 teaspoon garlic powder

½ cup sour cream

1 teaspoon chili powder

1 teaspoon onion salt

1 bunch green onions

3 medium red tomatoes

2 cups canned bean dip

1 cup sliced black olives

1 (8-ounce) package shredded Cheddar cheese

What You Do

1. Peel avocados and remove seeds. Mash together with lemon juice, salt, and garlic powder. Set aside.

2. Mix together sour cream, chili powder, and onion salt. Set aside.

3. Remove roots from green onions and chop into ½" pieces. Cut tomatoes into ½" pieces.

4. Layer on a large plate or platter in the following order: bean dip, avocado mix, sour cream mix, onion, tomatoes, olives, cheese.

5. Cover and chill in refrigerator for 4 hours before serving.

How Long Should I Cook Beans?

Any bean recipe gives you two options. Cook it longer and let the beans dissolve for a creamy texture. Serve it earlier in the cooking process, as soon as the beans are completely soft, for more distinct flavors in every bite. Be sure you never add salt before the beans have begun to soften or they will stay hard, no matter how long you cook them.

Jasmine & Rose Hips Tea v

Instead of using sugar, add a teaspoon of honey to each glass before serving.

What You Need

8 cups cold water

¼ pound jasmine flowers

¼ pound rose hips

½ cup sugar

What You Do

1. Place all ingredients in a glass container. Stir until sugar is dissolved.

2. Cover and set in a warm place for 6 to 8 hours.

3. Remove jasmine flowers and rose hips. Stir before serving.

What are Examples of Edible Flowers?

Most flowers are edible, although it is best to consult a horticulture book before gorging on your garden. Pansies, for example, are a delightful addition to a salad. Rose petals give a soft, rosy taste to water, unlike rose hips, which provide a tangy almost bitter flavoring.

Should I Use a Glass or Plastic Container?

Although many of today's drinking containers are made of plastic, glass or ceramic are the preferred containers when making an infused drink such as this. They stay cooler than plastic and don't leach any flavor into the water as many plastics can do.

In the United States we have Shirley Temples. In Mexico, kids get these fruity drinks while their elders are drinking, well, fruity drinks mixed with other things.

Angelina & José v

What You Need

1 Key lime

¾ cup sparkling water

1 tablespoon grenadine

¼ cup orange juice

What You Do

1. Cut the Key lime in half.

2. Combine the sparkling water, grenadine, and orange juice.

3. Squeeze the juice from half the Key lime into the drink and stir.

4. Use the other half of the lime as a garnish.

5. Serve over ice.

Of course, there's no rule that you can't add some tequila to this drink to create a fruity masterpiece.

Mock Sangria v

What You Need

1 orange

1 lemon

4 Key limes

6 cups purple grape juice

6 cups white grape juice

1 cup orange juice

½ cup lemon juice

What You Do

1. Cut the orange, lemon, and limes into ¼" rounds, retaining the rind.

2. Combine all ingredients in a large pitcher. Refrigerate for at least 4 hours before serving.

Tamarind-Ade v

Tamarind drinks are as popular in Mexico as lemonade is to the rest of North America. After trying this, you might make the switch.

What You Need

2 cups frozen or fresh tamarind pulp

· ½ cup brown sugar

2 cups water

What You Do

1. Combine all ingredients. Stir until sugar is dissolved.

2. Chill before serving.

?

What's Tamarind?

Tamarind is more commonly known as the main ingredient in Worcestershire sauce. In its original form, however, it is a dried brown seed pod. It produces a distinctive sour taste and many herbologists believe it can help the body break down fatty acids.

Hibiscus & Lime Water v

What You Need

8 cups cold water   ½ cup white sugar

1 cup dried hibiscus flowers   4 Key limes

What You Do

Combine the water, hibiscus flowers, and sugar in a glass container. Stir until sugar dissolves. Cut 3 limes in half and squeeze the juice into the water. Discard rinds. Cut the remaining lime into ¼" rounds and put in the water. Cover the container and store in a warm place for 6–12 hours. Strain to remove the hibiscus flowers and lime rounds before serving.

Sparkling Fruit Drink v

What You Need

4 cups watermelon meat   2 cups strawberries

1 mango   1 cup white sugar

1 papaya   2 gallons sparkling water

1 pineapple   2 pounds ice cubes

1 guava

What You Do

Remove the rind, stems, seeds, and cores from the fruits. Cut the fruit into ½" pieces. Reserve all juices. Stir the sugar into the water until it dissolves. Add the fruit and the juices to the water. Stir well. Add the ice cubes and serve immediately.

Green Almond Salsa v

This makes an excellent tostado chip dip but also can be used as a sauce when cooking chicken or pork.

What You Need

3 tablespoons olive oil

1 slice white bread

1 cup blanched almond slivers

½ can of tomatillos

½ cup green bell pepper

½ cup canned green jalapeño peppers

½ cup fresh cilantro

½ teaspoon dried coriander

½ teaspoon salt

½ teaspoon ground black pepper

1 teaspoon garlic paste

What You Do

1. Heat 2 tablespoons of the olive oil in a frying pan on medium-high heat. Fry the bread on both sides until it is medium brown. Set on paper towels to soak up remaining oil. When dry and cool, chop into ¼" pieces. Add remaining olive oil and almond slivers to skillet. Reduce heat to medium and cook almonds until they are medium brown. Drain the grease.

2. Cut the tomatillos into quarters. Remove the stem and seeds from the green bell pepper and cut into chunks. Drain the jalapeño peppers.

3. Add all ingredients to the blender or food processor. Blend on medium speed until all ingredients are well melded. Small pieces may remain. Pour into a saucepan and simmer on low heat for 10 minutes.

4. Refrigerate at least 4 hours before serving.

What are the Hottest Parts of a Chili Pepper?

The hottest parts of a chili pepper are the seeds and the pith, the fleshy interior that attaches to the seeds. The flesh contains less heat than the interior of the chili. Although chilies can be red, yellow, or green, the color is not an indication of how hot they are.

This is excellent as a basting sauce for swordfish or tuna steaks.

Crimson Prickly Pear Sauce v

What You Need

16 fresh prickly pears (avoid those with yellow-gray green rinds)

½ cup sugar

1 tablespoon lime juice

1 tablespoon orange liqueur

What You Do

1. Remove rind from prickly pears by cutting off both ends and running a slice down both sides. If ripe, the rind will pull off easily.

2. Chop prickly pear fruit into approximately 1" pieces and place in a blender. Blend on medium-high until you have a purée. Strain through cheesecloth or a fine strainer. Reserve both juice and purée. Remove seeds from purée.

3. Put 2 cups of prickly pear juice in a medium saucepan with ½ cup sugar. Cook over medium heat until mixture is reduced by half.

4. Remove from heat. Add 1 cup of puréed prickly pear, lime juice, and orange liqueur. Stir well.

5. Refrigerate for at least 4 hours before serving.

What Should I Know about Eating Cactus?

A prickly pear is an egg-shaped fruit that comes from the same prickly pear cactus that gives us the cactus paddles used as a vegetable. The flesh is watery and takes a bit like watermelon and strawberries although one variety (with yellow-gray green rinds) tastes sour. When ripe, the rind yields slightly to the touch. For those of us in northern climates, the idea of eating cactus is, well, terrifying. However, it is quite juicy and flavorful. Many people in the southwestern United States will simply pick their own backyard cactus. The canned variety is mushier and loses some of its flavor but is a good place to start for those new to this delicacy.

This makes an excellent condiment for grilled fish or chicken.

Jicama Salsa v

What You Need

1 medium carrot

1 small zucchini

½ cup fresh green beans

4 fresh radishes

1 medium white onion

2 tablespoons fresh cilantro leaves

1 medium jicama (about 2 pounds)

1 chipotle pepper

1 cup boiling water

½ teaspoon garlic powder

1 teaspoon dried oregano

½ cup white vinegar

½ cup water

½ cup olive oil

1 tablespoon lime juice

What You Do

1. Peel carrot and dice into ¼" pieces. Peel zucchini and dice into ¼" pieces. Snap ends off green beans and cut into ¼" pieces. Remove root and tops from radishes and cut into ¼" pieces. Peel onion and cut into ¼" pieces. Remove stems from cilantro and dice finely. Remove skin from jicama and dice into ¼" pieces.

2. Place green beans, chipotle pepper, carrots, and radishes in a small pot containing 1 cup boiling water. Cook for 2–3 minutes. Drain. Remove stem and seeds from pepper. Chop into ¼" pieces.

3. Mix all ingredients in a large mixing bowl. Cover and refrigerate for 4 hours. Let warm to room temperature before serving.

What's Paprika?

Paprika is made from red peppers, dried and powdered into a coarse-grained spice. It is used in many Spanish recipes and a handful of Mexican recipes. Paprika comes in many different strengths. The paprika that is typically sold in the United States is the most mild.

This is an excellent substitute for tomato salsa or even picante sauce, especially for people who prefer lots of garlic in their recipes

Garlic Salsa   v

What You Need

20 garlic cloves

1 small white onion

½ cup fresh parsley leaves

2 medium red tomatoes

1 fresh serrano pepper

½ teaspoon salt

½ teaspoon ground black pepper

½ teaspoon paprika

1 tablespoon dried oregano

Juice of 3 lemons

½ cup olive oil

What You Do

1. Peel garlic and mince. Peel onion and mince. Cut stems from parsley and mince leaves. Cut tomatoes into ¼" pieces. Remove stem and seeds from serrano pepper and cut into ¼" pieces.

2. Combine all ingredients. Mix well.

3. Cover and refrigerate for 8–12 hours before using.

?

What's Zucchini?

Zucchini is a wonderfully versatile squash that can be grown in almost any climate. It is good when small and still has many uses as it grows large. Many cooks use it instead of eggplant because it adds a subtle flavor and a great deal of substance to a dish. It also works much like tofu, soaking up the flavors of a dish.

Serve as an appetizer before any traditional Mexican meal, such as Mexican Pot Roast (see page 103).

Cabbage Tamales

What You Need

1 fresh cabbage

1 cup canned tomato soup

1 pound lean ground beef

1 pound patty sausage

1 cup dry rice

4 tablespoons chili powder

½ teaspoon salt

What You Do

1. Preheat oven to 300°F.

2. Cut core from cabbage. Separate leaves and place in a pan of warm water, making sure the water covers the leaves.

3. Combine canned soup, ground beef, sausage, rice, chili powder, and salt. Mix well with your hands so that all ingredients are blended.

4. Remove cabbage leaves from water and pat dry. Place about 2 tablespoons of meat mixture in the middle of each cabbage leaf. Roll up and secure with a toothpick.

5. Place rolls in a 9" × 12" baking dish. (It's all right to stack them.) Cover with aluminum foil. Bake for 1½ hours.

In addition to being used as an appetizer, these often are added to a basic Chicken Stock (see page 124), to make an interesting soup.

Spinach Balls

What You Need

3 eggs

½ cup Cheddar cheese

½ cup cooked ham

¼ cup flour

2 (10-ounce) packages frozen spinach, thawed

½ teaspoon salt

1 cup vegetable oil

What You Do

1. Separate eggs. Cut cheese into ½" cubes. Cut ham into ½" cubes.

2. Squeeze all liquid from thawed frozen spinach. Form into balls about the size of golf balls.

3. Push a piece of ham or cheese into the center of each ball.

4. Beat egg whites until stiff. Gradually beat in yolks, flour and salt. Coat spinach balls with egg batter.

5. Heat oil to medium-high. Fry one layer of spinach balls at a time until lightly browned.

When Should I Use a Slow Cooker?

Slow cookers are excellent appliances if you want to make a meal while you aren't at home or if you want to keep an appetizer warm for several hours. Soups and stews work well, as does any dish that doesn't require the food to brown and doesn't need to be quick-cooked, such as fried foods.

Serve with an assortment of salsas.

Cauliflower Tortas v

What You Need

1 head cauliflower

2 eggs

2 tablespoons flour

1 teaspoon salt

½ teaspoon ground black pepper

4 cups vegetable oil

What You Do

1. Rinse cauliflower, remove outer leaves, and separate into florets. Cook in boiling water until almost tender, 8–10 minutes. Drain.

2. Separate eggs. Beat egg whites until they form rounded peaks. Beat egg yolks until smooth. Pour yolks into whites gradually, beating lightly with a fork to combine.

3. In a separate small bowl, combine flour, salt, and pepper. Roll cooked cauliflower florets in the flour, then dip in eggs, coating well.

4. Heat oil to 375°F in a frying pan. Add a few cauliflower florets at a time. Fry until brown on all sides.

These are excellent served with any number of sauces and salsas.

Sweet Chilies Rellenos

What You Need

12–18 poblano peppers

1 small white onion

1 teaspoon capers

2 tablespoons candied lemon peel

¼ cup green olives

2 eggs

3 tablespoons shortening

1 pound lean ground pork

½ pound ground ham

¾ cup canned diced tomatoes

2 tablespoons parsley

½ teaspoon garlic paste

3 tablespoons cider vinegar

½ teaspoon vanilla extract

2 tablespoons sugar

¾ teaspoon ground cloves

¾ teaspoon black pepper

¼ teaspoon nutmeg

⅛ teaspoon powdered saffron

¼ cup slivered almonds

¼ cup seedless raisins

½ cup flour

Sweet Chilies Rellenos—continued

What You Do

1. Cut out stems of peppers. Remove seeds and membrane. Place peppers in a large saucepan. Cover with boiling water, bring to a boil, and cook about 2 minutes. Drain and invert peppers on a paper towel.

2. Peel onion and chop into ¼" pieces. Chop capers finely. Chop lemon peel finely. Chop green olives finely. Beat eggs and set aside.

3. Heat 3 tablespoons shortening in a large frying pan. Add onion and meat. Cook until meat is browned, stirring occasionally.

4. Mix tomatoes, parsley, garlic paste, vinegar, vanilla extract, sugar, cloves, pepper, nutmeg, and saffron. Add tomato mixture to meat along with almonds, raisins, capers, lemon peel, and olives. Stir. Cook over low heat, stirring frequently, until mixture is almost dry, about 30–40 minutes.

5. Spoon filling into peppers, packing lightly so mixture will remain in pepper cavities during frying.

6. Roll peppers in flour, coating entire surface. Dip in beaten eggs.

7. Heat oil to medium-high in a large frying pan. Fry peppers until golden. Place on paper towels to drain grease.

Roasted Morita Cream Sauce v

Serve warm over potatoes or fresh vegetables.

What You Need

½ cup whipping cream

½ cup plain yogurt

2 dried morita chilies

1 cup whole milk

2 tablespoons olive oil

1½ tablespoons flour

1 teaspoon salt

What You Do

1. Make thick cream by pouring the whipping cream into a small saucepan and cook on low heat until it is lukewarm. (It must not go above 100°F.)

2. Remove from heat and stir in plain yogurt. Pour into a clear glass jar covered with a loose cap or clear plastic food wrap. Place in a warm place (80°F to 90°F) such as the top of the refrigerator. Let the cream develop for 12–24 hours. Stir gently and chill 4–8 hours.

3. Remove stems and seeds from morita chilies and cut into 1" pieces.

4. Put chilies, salt, and milk in a food processor or blender. Blend on medium setting until smooth. Heat the milk and chili mixture in a medium saucepan over medium-low heat.

5. In another saucepan, blend the olive oil and flour. Cook over medium heat, stirring constantly for 2 to 3 minutes. After about 3 minutes, begin gently whisking in the heated milk and chili mixture. Continue to cook and stir until smooth and thickened.

6. Whisk in the thick cream.

Chapter 3

Soups, Stews, and Moles

Jalapeño Potato Soup

Add a dollop of sour cream and sprigs of fresh cilantro before serving.

What You Need

1 medium yellow onion

5 pounds red potatoes

¼ cup butter

8 cups chicken broth (see Chicken Stock, page 124)

1 teaspoon cumin

¼ cup fresh (or ⅛ cup canned) sliced jalapeño peppers

¼ teaspoon baking soda

4 cups evaporated milk

½ teaspoon ground black pepper

What You Do

1. Remove skin from onion and cut into ¼" pieces. Clean potatoes and cut into quarters. (Do not peel the potatoes.)

2. Cook onions in butter until clear but not brown.

3. Put potatoes and onions into a large stock pot. Add chicken broth and cumin. Cook uncovered about 30 minutes until potatoes are tender.

4. Coarsely mash potatoes with a potato masher. Stir in jalapeños, baking soda, black pepper, and evaporated milk. Stir well.

5. Simmer on low heat for 15 minutes, stirring constantly.

Mexican Onion Soup

Serve with Brie and Papaya Quesadillas (see page 30) for a light yet filling lunch.

What You Need

3 large yellow onions

¼ cup butter

2 cups tomato juice

2 cups beef broth (canned or homemade)

½ teaspoon garlic paste

1 cup water

½ cup basic tomato salsa (see Tomato Salsa, page 12)

1 cup Monterey jack cheese

What You Do

1. Remove skins from onions and slice into thin rings.

2. Melt butter over low heat in a large frying pan. Add onions and cook for about 20 minutes, stirring frequently. Onions should be tender and light brown.

3. Stir in tomato juice, beef broth, garlic paste, water, and salsa. Bring to a boil. Reduce heat to low.

4. Simmer uncovered for 20 minutes. Top with grated cheese before serving.

Asparagus & Pistachio Soup

LEVEL **E**

SERVINGS **8**

If reheating this soup, make sure it never comes to a boil because the cream will turn brown.

Serve with warm flour tortillas and fresh butter.

What You Need

1 medium onion

2 cups asparagus tips, 1" long

½ cup natural pistachio meats

1 tablespoon butter

6 cups chicken broth (see Chicken Stock, page 124)

½ teaspoon salt

1 teaspoon ground black pepper

¼ cup cooking sherry

½ cup heavy cream

What You Do

1. Remove skin from onion and chop into ¼" pieces.

2. Cook asparagus tips in water on medium heat until slightly tender.

3. Cover pistachio meats with boiling water and let sit for 10 minutes. Remove the skins and let the meats dry. Cook the pistachio meats in butter on medium heat until golden. Set the pistachio meats aside and add the onion to the butter. Cook until limp.

5. Combine 1 cup of chicken broth, pistachio meats, onion, salt, black pepper, and cooking sherry in a blender and stir until they form a smooth paste.

6. Place mixture in a medium-sized pot on medium heat. Add remaining chicken broth. Stir until well mixed. Add asparagus tips and cook for 20 minutes on low heat. Stir in cream right before serving.

What Should I Know About Choosing Pistachios?

Pistachios are a common treat in Mexico. When walking the streets of virtually any town, you're likely to have a child come up to you offering fresh roasted pistachios. Be sure to avoid the red and white dyed pistachios sold in the United States as the dye will discolor your food.

An alternative for cooking this soup is to put all the ingredients except the lime juice, tostada, and cilantro in a slow cooker, cover, and cook on low setting for 8–10 hours.

Then add the lime juice and sprinkle with tostada pieces and cilantro.

Chicken Tortilla Soup

What You Need

1 medium white onion

1 red bell pepper

2 cups cubed cooked chicken

2 tablespoons chili powder

2 teaspoons salt

1 tablespoon ground cumin

½ teaspoon ground red pepper

6 cups chicken broth (canned or fresh)

1 (14½ ounce) can diced tomatoes

2 cups canned (and drained) or frozen corn

3 cups cooked black beans

1 teaspoon garlic paste

1 teaspoon sugar

¼ cup lime juice

4 Tostadas (see page 287)

1 bunch fresh cilantro leaves

What You Do

1. Remove skin from onion. Chop onion into ¼" pieces. Remove stem and core from red bell pepper and chop into ¼" pieces.

2. Combine all ingredients except lime juice, tostadas, and cilantro in a soup pot. Bring to a boil and cook for 20 minutes. Reduce heat to low, cover, and simmer for 2 hours. Stir in lime juice before serving.

3. Break tostadas into small pieces. Cut stems from cilantro. Sprinkle tostada pieces and cilantro leaves on soup before serving.

Roasted Pepper & Cabbage Soup

Make this a heartier meal by adding two cups of dry white rice to the soup before simmering.

You can substitute canned (and drained) corn for the frozen corn.

What You Need

2 red bell peppers

1 tablespoon olive oil

1 large white onion

2 large carrots

1 medium cabbage

2 medium zucchini (8" to 12" long)

2 cups frozen corn

1 teaspoon garlic paste

2 teaspoons salt

1 teaspoon black pepper

6 cups canned or fresh chicken broth (see Chicken Stock, page 124)

What You Do

1. Preheat oven to 350°F.

2. Remove stems and seeds from red bell peppers. Cut peppers into 2" wide strips. Place skin-side-down on a cookie sheet. Spread olive oil over the pepper strips. Place in oven and bake for 30 minutes or until peppers are lightly blackened on the edges.

3. Remove skin from onion and chop into ¼" pieces. Clean carrots and chop into ¼" rounds. Tear cabbage leaves into pieces about 3" square. Clean zucchini and cut into ½" pieces. Cut red pepper pieces into 1" squares.

4. Add all ingredients to a large stock pot. Bring to a boil, cover, and cook for 20 minutes. Reduce heat to medium-low and simmer for 2 hours.

Where Are the Hot Peppers?

While many people think Mexican food must have hot chili pepper in it to be traditional, that is absolutely not true. Mexican food is known for its use of fresh fruits and vegetables and a variety of spices, both mild and unusual. Hot peppers are just one of many interesting things to discover with this cuisine.

LEVEL **E**

SERVINGS **6**

This makes a wonderful summer lunch served with a fresh fruit salad.

Cold Avocado Soup

What You Need

1 medium yellow onion

2 ripe avocados

4 cups chicken broth (see Chicken Stock, page 124)

1 medium canned tomatillo

½ cup fresh cilantro leaves

¼ cup canned jalapeño peppers

¾ teaspoon garlic paste

1 teaspoon salt

½ teaspoon ground red pepper

1 cup sour cream

¼ cup lime juice

What You Do

1. Remove skin from onion and quarter. Remove skin and pits from avocados then cut into 2" pieces. Combine all ingredients except sour cream and lime juice in a food processor or blender. You may need to do 2 or 3 batches. Blend on medium setting until ingredients are well melded and smooth.

2. Refrigerate for 3 hours. Remove any fat that has congealed on the top of the soup. Stir and refrigerate for an additional hour. Top with a dollop of sour cream and a sprinkle of lime juice before serving.

?

What's an Avocado?

An avocado actually is a fruit that comes in several different varieties. It is fairly high in calories (about 300 for an average avocado). Although many people think otherwise, avocados contain only monounsaturated fat, the good kind of cholesterol. When choosing a ripe avocado, the flesh should give slightly to your touch.

Creamy Corn Soup

Garnish with strips of roasted red peppers to create a festive look and a unique combination of flavors.

What You Need

1 large white onion

3 cups frozen or canned (and drained) whole-kernel corn

1 (14-ounce) can diced tomatoes, drained

4 cups chicken broth (see Chicken Stock, page 124)

1 teaspoon salt

½ teaspoon ground black pepper

1 cup whipping cream

What You Do

1. Remove skin from onion and cut into quarters.

2. Put corn, onion, tomatoes, and 1 cup of chicken broth in a food processor or blender. Blend on medium setting until all ingredients are melded. They do not have to be liquefied—small pieces of corn, onion, and tomato are fine.

3. Place remaining chicken broth in a large saucepan on medium-low heat. Stir in blended mixture. Add salt and pepper. Heat thoroughly but do not boil.

4. Stir in whipping cream and cook on low heat, stirring constantly, for 5 minutes.

Spicy Vegetable Soup

Serve this soup with Jalapeño Corn Bread (see page 184).

You can substitute canned (and drained) green beans for the frozen green beans. This goes for the peas and corn as well.

What You Need

2 large carrots

1 large yellow onion

2 celery ribs

2 medium zucchini (8" to 10" long)

1 pound fresh spinach

½ red bell pepper

2 medium potatoes

8 cups chicken broth (see Chicken Stock, page 124)

2 cups frozen green beans

1 (14½ ounce) can diced tomatoes

1 cup frozen peas

1 cup frozen corn

¼ cup canned sliced chili peppers

1 teaspoon salt

½ teaspoon ground red pepper

½ teaspoon chili powder

1 teaspoon garlic paste

4 tablespoons vegetable oil

What You Do

1. Peel carrots and cut into ¼" rounds. Remove skin from onion and cut into ¼" pieces. Cut celery into ¼" pieces. Cut zucchini into 1" pieces. Remove stems from spinach. Remove stem and seeds from red bell pepper and cut half the pepper into ¼" pieces. Peel potatoes and cut into 1" pieces.

2. Put chicken broth in a large stock pot on high heat. Add remaining ingredients to pot. Stir well. Bring to a boil. Cover and reduce heat to medium.

3. Simmer for 2 to 3 hours.

This is a great way to use leftover turkey. It also works well with chicken.

Turkey & Filbert Soup

What You Need

1 medium white onion

½ cup filberts

2 cups diced cooked turkey

8 cups chicken broth (see Chicken Stock, page 124)

¼ cup butter

½ teaspoon nutmeg

1 tablespoon dried parsley flakes

1 teaspoon salt

1 teaspoon ground black pepper

¼ cup dry red wine

What You Do

1. Remove skin from onion and chop into ¼" pieces.

2. Melt butter in a small frying pan at medium heat and cook filberts for 5 minutes. Drain butter and discard.

3. Place filberts, ½ cup turkey meat, onions, and 1 cup of chicken broth in blender or food processor. Blend at medium speed until you have a purée—you should have a thick substance with all ingredients melded.

4. Add the mixture to the remaining chicken broth and place in a large stock pot. Add the remaining ingredients. Heat on medium setting for 30 minutes, stirring frequently.

Serve with Jalapeño Corn Bread (see page 184).

Mexican Chicken Chowder

What You Need

1½ pounds boneless, skinless chicken breasts

2 medium white onions

2 celery ribs

½ teaspoon garlic paste

1 tablespoon olive oil

4 cups chicken broth (see Chicken Stock, page 124)

1 (1-ounce) package dry chicken gravy mix

2 cups whole milk

2 cups tomato salsa (see Tomato Salsa, page 12)

1 (32-ounce) bag frozen hash brown potatoes

½ cup canned, chopped jalapeño peppers

1 (8-ounce) package shredded Cheddar or Colby cheese

What You Do

1. Preheat oven to 300°F.

2. Cut the chicken into ½" cubes. Peel the onions and cut into ¼" pieces. Cut the celery into ¼" pieces.

3. Combine the chicken, onions, garlic, celery, oil, and broth in a large mixing bowl. Stir until well blended. Pour into a casserole dish. Cover and put in oven for 1 hour.

4. Dissolve the gravy mix in the milk in a medium mixing bowl. Stir into the chicken mixture. Add the salsa, potatoes, peppers, and cheese. Mix well. Cover and cook for an additional hour.

When Should I Add the Salt?

Resist the urge to salt. Salt draws flavors and juices out of meat and vegetables. Let the flavors release on their own time for the best results. Guests can salt their own dishes if they prefer. They'll also use less than if you add it while cooking.

Market Basket Soup

This soup is also called wastebasket soup, probably because it is often made at the end of the week when the refrigerator and cupboards are being cleaned out.

What You Need

2 pounds smoky link sausages

1 small white onion

2 celery ribs

1 green bell pepper

1 medium zucchini (8" to 12" long)

¼ cup canned jalapeño peppers

2 cups canned pinto beans

1 cup canned or frozen whole kernel corn

1 (14-ounce) can diced tomatoes

1 (4-ounce) package Bloody Mary mix

1 cup canned or frozen green lima beans

1 (1-ounce) package dry onion soup mix

1 cup sliced black olives

2 cups water

2 teaspoons salt

2 teaspoons ground white pepper

1 teaspoon ground oregano

What You Do

Cook sausages in a medium frying pan at medium-low heat until lightly browned. Cut into 1" pieces. Peel onion and chop into ¼" pieces. Cut celery into ¼" pieces. Remove stem and seeds from green bell pepper and cut into ¼" pieces. Cut zucchini into 1" pieces. Add all ingredients to a large soup pot. Stir well. Bring to a boil then lower temperature to medium-low and simmer uncovered for 1 hour.

How Can I Lower the Cholesterol of a Recipe?

When frying, cooking, or browning foods, you don't have to use oil. Many chefs simply use a little bit of water to cook these items. When browning a fatty meat, such as sausages, start cooking them at a low temperature to cook some of the fat out before you turn up the temperature for browning.

Use as an appetizer for a heavier meal or as the main course for a summer luncheon.

Gazpacho with Avocado v

What You Need

4 hardboiled eggs

5 medium red tomatoes

1 large cucumber

1 medium white onion

1 ripe avocado

¼ cup vegetable oil

1 tablespoon prepared yellow mustard

1 tablespoon Worcestershire sauce

¼ cup lime juice

1 teaspoon garlic salt

½ teaspoon ground black pepper

1 cup sour cream

What You Do

1. Peel and slice eggs in half, removing yolk. Set whites aside. Set 1 tomato aside and chop 4 into quarters. Pare and seed cucumber. Chop ¾ into 1" pieces. Peel onion and cut into quarters. Peel avocado and remove pit. Set aside half.

2. Put 4 chopped tomatoes, ¾ of cucumber, onion, and ½ of avocado in blender or food processor. Blend until smooth.

3. Put egg yolks in a small bowl and mash with a fork. Blend in oil, mustard, Worcestershire sauce, lime juice, garlic salt, and pepper. Add mixture to blender and blend until thoroughly mixed. Add sour cream gradually, blending well.

4. Pour mixture into a medium container with cover. Chop remaining tomato, cucumber, and hardboiled egg whites and add to soup. Slice remaining avocado half thinly and add to soup. Stir in lightly.

5. Cover and refrigerate at least 8 hours before serving.

Beef & Cactus Stew

This is excellent served with Red Rice (see page 212).

What You Need

2 pounds cubed beef

2 tablespoons olive oil

1 medium yellow onion

1 cup canned cactus pieces, drained

4 canned tomatillos, drained

4 garlic cloves

¼ cup canned sliced jalapeños, drained

2 chipotle peppers

1 cup canned diced tomatoes

1 teaspoon garlic paste

1 teaspoon oregano

1 teaspoon salt

1 teaspoon ground black pepper

What You Do

1. Place beef in a frying pan with the olive oil. Heat to medium temperature. Cook until brown on all sides.

2. Remove skin from onion and cut into 1" pieces. Cut cactus into 1" pieces. Cut tomatillos into 1" pieces.

3. Add all ingredients to the beef. Reduce heat to low. Cover and cook for 1 hour, stirring periodically.

?

What Oil to Use?

In most recipes you can substitute virgin olive oil for the vegetable oil. It gives a slightly more tangy taste. Sunflower and soy oil have the lightest flavors and are the healthiest. Corn oil is slightly heavy and gives a heartier feel to a dish. Traditionally, Mexican cooking uses lard, which adds a beefy flavor but contributes to heart disease.

Chicken Dry Soup

What You Need

4 boneless, skinless chicken breasts

1 medium yellow onion

1 tablespoon olive oil

½ teaspoon garlic paste

1 cup tomato salsa

4 cups chicken broth (see Chicken Stock, page 124)

5 corn tortillas

What You Do

1. Cut chicken breasts into 1" cubes. Remove skin from onion and cut into ¼" pieces.

2. Put olive oil in a large frying pan on medium heat. Put chicken, onion, and garlic paste in frying pan and cook until chicken is brown on all sides.

3. Reduce heat to low and add salsa and chicken broth. Mix well. Cook for 30 minutes uncovered, stirring periodically.

4. Tear tortillas into 1" pieces. Add to frying pan. Stir well. Cover and simmer for 1 hour.

5. Remove cover and simmer until dish is moist but not runny.

Mexican Chicken Casserole

Serve over a bed of lettuce with fresh Tostadas (see page 287).

What You Need

4 boneless, skinless chicken breasts

1 small onion

12 flour tortillas (see Flour Tortillas, page 286)

1½ cups shredded Cheddar cheese

1 (10¾-ounce) can cream of mushroom condensed soup

1 (10¾-ounce) can cream of chicken condensed soup

1 cup sour cream

½ cup canned chopped jalapeño peppers

1 cup tomato salsa (see Tomato Salsa, page 12)

What You Do

1. Preheat oven to 300°F.

2. Cut chicken into 1" cubes. Peel the onion and grate using the fine side of a vegetable grater. Tear the tortillas into eighths.

3. Combine the onion, cheese, soups, sour cream, and jalapeño peppers in a medium-sized bowl. Make layers in a casserole dish using a third of the corn tortillas, soup mixture, chicken, then salsa. Repeat twice

4. Cover and bake for 2 hours.

Beef & Bean Stew

Serve with white rice and a fresh fruit salad.

What You Need

1 yellow onion

4 red tomatoes

1 beef bouillon cube

2 pounds cubed beef

¼ teaspoon ground black pepper

½ teaspoon garlic salt

1 tablespoon chili powder

1 tablespoon prepared yellow mustard

½ cup canned chopped jalapeño peppers, drained

2 cups canned kidney beans, drained

What You Do

1. Peel and chop the onion into ¼" pieces. Cut the tomatoes into quarters. Crush the bouillon cube.

2. Mix meat, pepper, garlic salt, chili powder, and mustard in a large pot. Cover with onion, crushed bouillon cube, tomatoes, jalapeño peppers, and beans. Mix well.

3. Cover and cook on medium-low temperature for 2 hours. Stir periodically.

What Type of Tomato Should I Cook With?

All tomatoes are not alike. Substitute plum tomatoes for a more robust flavor. Choose golden tomatoes for a more mellow taste. Reserve pricier hothouse tomatoes for recipes in which tomatoes are the main ingredient.

Beef Picadillo

This is excellent served with Broccoli Salad (see page 87).

What You Need

1 small white onion

1 medium apple

1 pound ground beef

½ teaspoon garlic paste

1 cup canned or fresh tomato sauce

½ cup raisins

¼ cup toasted almond slivers

1 tablespoon vinegar

1 teaspoon sugar

1 teaspoon salt

¼ teaspoon cinnamon

¼ teaspoon cumin

⅛ teaspoon ground black pepper

What You Do

1. Peel onion and cut into ¼" pieces. Peel and remove core and stem from apple. Cut into ¼" pieces.

2. Place ground beef, garlic, and onion in a medium frying pan. Cook on medium heat, stirring to break up meat, until ground beef is browned.

3. Stir in tomato sauce, apple, raisins, almond slivers, vinegar, sugar, salt, cinnamon, cumin, and pepper.

4. Continue cooking on medium heat, stirring periodically, until all ingredients are well blended.

Caldo de Rez

Serve with
Pineapple Coconut
Salad
(see page 94).

What You Need

1 medium cabbage

1 small white onion

1 celery rib

4 medium baking potatoes

1½ pounds cubed stew beef

⅓ cup chopped frozen green pepper

1 teaspoon dried cilantro

1 (14½-ounce) can diced tomatoes

1 teaspoon salt

½ teaspoon ground black pepper

1 teaspoon Tabasco or other hot sauce

What You Do

1. Cut cabbage into wedges. Peel onion and chop into ¼" pieces. Chop celery rib into ¼" pieces. Peel potatoes and cut into 1" cubes.

2. Place all ingredients into a large pot. Stir until well mixed. Cover, bring to a boil, reduce temperature to medium-low, and simmer for 30 minutes.

What If a Dish Tastes Too Salty?

If the dish tastes too salty, add a teaspoon each of cider vinegar and sugar to the recipe. They will neutralize the salt without adding additional flavor.

Cashew Chili v

Because the nuts provide all the protein, you don't need meat to have a complete meal.

Serve with a side of fresh fruit.

What You Need

1 medium white onion

1 small green bell pepper

2 celery ribs

1 tablespoon vegetable oil

1 teaspoon oregano

1 teaspoon cumin

1 teaspoon garlic powder

1 tablespoon chili powder

1 (14½-ounce) can diced tomatoes

4 cups canned kidney beans

2 cups cashews

What You Do

1. Peel onion and cut into ¼" pieces. Remove seeds and stem from green pepper and cut into ¼" pieces. Cut celery into ¼" pieces.

2. Heat vegetable oil to medium temperature in a medium skillet. Add chopped onion, green pepper, and celery. Cook until onion is browned. Add oregano, cumin, garlic powder, and chili powder. Stir well.

3. Transfer mixture to a soup kettle. Add kidney beans and tomatoes. Simmer on low for 3 hours, stirring periodically. Add cashews and heat through just before serving.

Should I Use Garlic Cloves, Paste, or Powder?

Since this is a cookbook designed to keep things as easy as possible, it usually calls for garlic paste, which can be bought by the jar. You can substitute fresh cloves of garlic, removing their skins and chopping them finely or crushing them into your own paste with a garlic press. Or, you can substitute in the other direction, with garlic powder. In dishes that require cooking, especially long cooking, the flavor will not differ significantly. In the few recipes where only fresh garlic cloves should be used, they are specified.

Use flour tortillas for a slightly different taste.

Tomato Dry Soup v

What You Need

1 large white onion

10–12 stale corn tortillas

½ cup vegetable oil

½ teaspoon garlic paste

2 cups canned tomatoes with juice

1 teaspoon salt

½ teaspoon ground black pepper

½ teaspoon oregano

1 cup whipping cream

1 cup shredded Parmesan cheese

1 teaspoon paprika

What You Do

1. Preheat oven to 350°F.

2. Peel onion and chop into ¼" pieces. Cut tortillas into ½"-wide strips. Heat 2 tablespoons of oil in a large saucepan to medium temperature. Add onion and garlic. Cook until onion is soft but not brown. Add undrained tomatoes, salt, pepper, and oregano and stir until blended. Heat to simmering and cook about 10 minutes.

4. Heat remaining oil in a large frying pan. Fry tortilla strips until limp, not crisp. Set on paper towels to drain grease.

5. In an ovenproof casserole, arrange layers as follows: tomato sauce, tortilla strips, cream, then cheese. Repeat until all ingredients are used, ending with cheese. Sprinkle paprika on top. Bake for 20 minutes uncovered or until dish is bubbling.

Cornball Soup

This can also be made using a beef stock with beef and vegetable chunks.

What You Need

1 small yellow onion

2 cups regular cornmeal

1 cup milk

2 eggs

¼ teaspoon garlic paste

¼ cup grated fresh Parmesan cheese

1 tablespoon crushed fresh cilantro

1 cup diced canned tomatoes

¼ cup vegetable oil

8 cups chicken broth (see Chicken Stock, page 124)

2 teaspoons salt

1 teaspoon ground black pepper

What You Do

1. Remove skin from onion and mince.

2. Combine cornmeal, milk, eggs, onion, garlic, Parmesan cheese, and cilantro. Roll into balls about the size of golf balls.

3. Put tomatoes in blender or food processor and blend on medium setting until thick and creamy.

4. Put vegetable oil in a medium frying pan on medium-high heat. Add cornmeal balls and fry until lightly brown. (Cut one open to make sure they are cooked in the center.) Keep them warm by putting them in a warm oven.

5. Heat chicken broth. Stir in tomato purée, salt, and black pepper. Add cornmeal balls. Serve immediately.

?

What is the Origin of Cornball Soup?

It's interesting how soups travel through different cultures, changing to fit the available ingredients and tastes of different peoples. This soup seems awfully similar to Matzo ball soup, yet it has a distinctly Mexican touch with the tomatoes, cilantro, and garlic.

Beef Stew

When fresh vegetables are in season, don't hesitate to add carrots, corn, or any of your favorite vegetables to this dish.

What You Need

3 fresh jalapeño peppers

2 medium white onions

2 garlic cloves

3 medium red tomatoes

3 tablespoons vegetable oil

4 medium potatoes

1 medium zucchini (about 10" long)

3 pounds cooked beef

2 teaspoons salt

1 teaspoon ground black pepper

What You Do

1. Remove stems and seeds from jalapeños and cut into quarters. Remove skin from onions and cut into quarters. Remove skin from garlic cloves. Cut tomatoes into quarters. Place these ingredients in blender or food processor and blend on medium until all ingredients are puréed. They should look as though they are chopped into very small pieces, but not blended into a paste.

2. Heat the oil on medium-high setting in a large frying pan. Add the purée and cook, stirring constantly, for 5 minutes.

3. Peel potatoes and cut into 1" cubes. Place in a medium saucepan, cover with water, and boil until tender. Drain and set aside. Cut zucchini into 1" cubes. Combine all ingredients in frying pan. Stir gently. Heat on medium setting for 10 minutes.

Can You Really Eat a Mole?

Moles (pronounced mo-LAY) are actually thick, intensely flavorful sauces, usually featuring different chili peppers, chocolate, and nuts. Sometimes the mole is poured over uncut pieces of meat, such as chicken breasts so the meat can stew that way. Most often, however, the meat is cut up and made part of the sauce.

Serve with a
fruit salad for a
complete meal.

Pork Pozole

What You Need

4 medium yellow onions

1 (14½-ounce) can diced tomatoes

½ cup canned sliced peppers (jalapeño or serrano)

4 pounds lean pork roast

2 pounds fresh or frozen hominy

1 teaspoon garlic paste

¼ cup sugar

3 tablespoons salt

1 teaspoon ground black pepper

2 cups tomato sauce

2 tablespoons lemon juice

What You Do

1. Peel onions and chop into ¼" pieces. Cut tomatoes into ¼" pieces. Remove stems and seeds from chili peppers.

2. In a large stew pot, combine the roast, hominy, garlic, onions, sugar, salt, black pepper, and jalapeño or serrano peppers. Cover with water, bring to a boil, turn heat to medium-low, and cook until the meat is done and the hominy is tender but not mushy, about 3 hours. Stir occasionally and add more water if necessary.

3. Remove meat and shred. Return the meat to the pot. Add tomatoes and tomato sauce. Cook uncovered at medium temperature for 30 minutes. Stir in lemon juice right before serving.

What's *Pozole*?

Mexican cooking has many dishes with no European equivalents. Although this is a stew because many ingredients are mixed with liquids, pozole tends to be heavier and thicker than a traditional stew. If the hominy is not overcooked, it also will be a bit crunchy, adding a unique texture to what most North Americans think of in a stew.

Pigs Feet Stew

Serve with fresh chilies, limes, lettuce, onion, and radishes to add to the soup as garnishes.

If you want to be truly authentic, you can remove the cooked meat from the pigs feet to add to the cubed pork in the stew.

What You Need

8 garlic cloves

3 medium potatoes

1 large white onion

3 medium carrots

6 pigs feet

1 teaspoon salt

1 teaspoon oregano

1 pound cubed pork

1 cup canned or frozen peas, drained or thawed

What You Do

1. Peel garlic and slice thinly. Peel potatoes and cut into 1" cubes. Peel onion and chop into ¼" pieces. Peel carrots and cut into ¼" rounds.

2. Put pigs feet and onion into a large stock pot with water. Add salt and oregano. Stir well. Bring to a boil. Boil uncovered 30 minutes.

3. Add remaining ingredients. Reduce heat to medium and simmer uncovered 3–4 hours or until carrots are soft and meat is tender.

Do I Need a Food Processor?

As with all electrical gadgets, a food processor simply saves time. Several decades ago, our grandmothers achieved the same—and sometimes better—dishes by cutting, grinding, and mashing by hand. Remember, you never have to use a food processor, blender, or nut grinder. Just count on it taking more time if you don't.

Mole Poblano

Use as a sauce for poultry or red meat. Use as a filling for tortillas or tamales by adding three cups of chopped, precooked chicken, beef, or turkey to the sauce and warming it thoroughly.

What You Need

6 dried ancho chilies

1 large onion

1 garlic clove

1 corn tortilla (see Basic Corn Tortillas, page 285)

2 cups canned tomatoes

½ cup salted peanuts

⅓ cup raisins

2 tablespoons sesame seeds

¼ cup oil

1 tablespoon sugar

¼ teaspoon ground anise

¼ teaspoon ground cinnamon

¼ teaspoon ground cloves

¼ teaspoon ground coriander

¼ teaspoon ground cumin

1 cup chicken broth (see Chicken Stock, page 124)

1 (1-ounce) package unsweetened dark chocolate, grated

1 teaspoon salt

1 teaspoon ground black pepper

Mole Poblano—*continued*

What You Do

1. Break off stems and shake out seeds from ancho chilies. Peel onion and quarter. Peel garlic and quarter. Tear tortilla into 1" pieces.

2. Combine chilies, onion, garlic, tomatoes with their juice, peanuts, tortilla, raisins, and sesame seeds in a blender. Blend on medium speed until you have a thick purée.

3. Heat oil to medium temperature in a large frying pan. Add the purée and cook, stirring constantly, for about 5 minutes. Stir in sugar, anise, cinnamon, cloves, coriander, cumin, and chicken broth. Bring to a boil. Reduce heat to low and simmer uncovered for 10 minutes.

4. Add chocolate and continue simmering, stirring constantly, until the chocolate is melted and blended into the sauce. Add salt and pepper.

What is the Origin of Mole Poblano?

Legend has it that the nuns of Santa Rosa received a surprise visit from their archbishop in the late 1500s. They had little time to prepare dinner for such an esteemed guest so they added everything in their kitchen to their mole sauce. Today, this is one of the most famous—and most used—sauces in Mexican cooking.

Mexican Meatball Stew

Serve with fresh Basic Corn Tortillas (see page 285), and Tomato Salsa (see page 12).

What You Need

1 large white onion

6 carrots

6 new potatoes (small)

2 large jalapeño peppers

1½ pounds lean ground beef

½ pound ground sausage

1 teaspoon dried cilantro

1 teaspoon salt

1 teaspoon black pepper

1 teaspoon cumin

1 teaspoon celery salt

1 teaspoon garlic powder

2 tablespoons vegetable oil

6 cups water

1 cup canned hominy

1 15-ounce can red kidney beans

3 beef bouillon cubes

1 14½ ounce can diced tomatoes

What You Do

1. Peel onion and cut into ¼" pieces. Peel carrots and cut into quarters. Wash potatoes and quarter. Remove stems and seeds from jalapeño peppers and cut into ¼" rounds.

2. Combine ground beef and ground sausage. Add cilantro, salt, black pepper, cumin, celery salt, and garlic powder. Mix well with your hands. Form meatballs slightly smaller than golf balls.

3. Heat oil in a skillet at medium-high heat. Add meatballs and garlic to taste. Cook until browned, flipping meatballs so all sides are browned. Drain grease. Set meatballs on paper towels to soak up excess grease.

4. Transfer to a large stew pot. Add water, potatoes, carrots, onions, jalapeño peppers, hominy, and kidney beans. Cook 1 hour on medium-low heat or until potatoes and carrots are tender.

5. Add beef bouillon cubes and tomatoes.

Chapter 4
Salads

Cucumber Mousse v

Use as the salad
course when serving
Chicken Tablecloth
Stainer (see page
149).

What You Need

1 small white onion

1 medium cucumber

1 (3-ounce) package lime-flavored gelatin

¾ cup boiling water

1 cup cottage cheese

1 cup mayonnaise

1 cup slivered almonds

What You Do

1. Peel onion and grate until you have 2 tablespoons.
   Grate cucumber until you have ¾ cup.

2. Dissolve gelatin in boiling water. Stir in cottage
   cheese, mayonnaise, and onion until well blended.

3. Fold in cucumber and almonds.

4. Pour mixture into a 1-quart mold. Refrigerate until
   set.

Shrimp Salad

This works well as a main course, especially for lunch.

Serve with Jalapeño Corn Bread (see page 184).

What You Need

3 hardboiled eggs

1 small white onion

1 bunch fresh cilantro

2 large red tomatoes

½ cup green olives stuffed with pimientos

1 avocado

¼ cup lime juice

½ cup olive oil

1 teaspoon salt

1 teaspoon ground black pepper

3 cups cooked baby shrimp

What You Do

1. Peel eggs and chop into small pieces.

2. Remove skin from onion and chop into ¼" pieces. Remove stems from cilantro and chop leaves roughly. Chop tomatoes into ½" pieces. Chop olives into quarters. Peel avocado, discard pit, and chop into ½" pieces.

3. Combine lime juice, olive oil, salt, and pepper. Mix well.

4. Combine shrimp, onion, eggs, avocado, cilantro, tomatoes, and olives in a large mixing bowl. Pour lime juice and olive oil dressing over the top. Stir gently until ingredients are well blended.

5. Chill before serving.

You can easily turn this into a mixed seafood salad by adding cooked shrimp, lobster meat, and scallops.

Crab Salad

What You Need

2 cups precooked crab meat

1 medium jicama

1 celery rib

1 cup cucumber

1 small white onion

1 fresh jalapeño pepper

⅓ cup mayonnaise

⅓ cup sour cream

½ cup sliced black olives

1 teaspoon salt

1 teaspoon cayenne pepper

What You Do

1. Shred crab meat. Peel jicama and cut into ½" pieces. Cut celery into ¼" pieces. Peel cucumber and cut into ½" pieces. Remove skin from onion and cut into ¼" pieces. Remove stem and seeds from jalapeño pepper and cut into ¼" pieces.

2. Mix mayonnaise and sour cream together.

3. Combine crab meat, jicama, celery, cucumber, black olives, onion, jalapeño pepper, salt, and cayenne pepper in a mixing bowl. Add mayonnaise and sour cream mixture. Mix until blended. Serve chilled.

? ## What's Jicama?

Jicama is a root vegetable with a crisp, white flesh. It has a very mild flavor that will pick up the flavor of dressings or spices. It's an excellent addition to salads because it looks so beautiful nestled among all the other colored foods!

Try making this salad with any fresh vegetables, such as green beans, broccoli, or even carrots.

Fresh Cauliflower Salad

What You Need

1 head cauliflower

2 celery ribs

1 large red onion

6 slices bacon

1 cup tomato salsa (see Tomato Salsa, page 12)

1 teaspoon salt

1 teaspoon cumin

½ cup sour cream

What You Do

1. Break cauliflower florets into bite-size pieces. Wash celery and slice into ⅛" thick slices. Peel onion and chop into ¼" pieces. Cook bacon until crisp. Drain bacon grease and discard. Crumble bacon.

2. Combine ½ cup salsa, salt, and cumin. Add cauliflower florets, celery, onion, and bacon. Mix well. Chill in covered container for at least 2 hours.

3. Right before serving, combine the sour cream and remaining ½ cup salsa Pour over vegetable mixtures and toss lightly.

Black Bean & Corn Salad v

You can add more peppers to this to give it more spiciness.

Also try adding fresh green beans and carrots when they're in season.

What You Need

1 red bell pepper

1 fresh habanero pepper

1 medium Vidalia onion

1 celery rib

¼ cup sour cream

¼ cup mayonnaise

2 15-ounce cans black beans, drained

2 15-ounce cans kernel corn, drained

What You Do

1. Remove stem and seeds from red bell pepper and cut into ½" pieces. Remove stem and seeds from habanero pepper and cut into ¼" pieces. Remove skin from Vidalia onion and cut into ½" pieces. Cut celery into ¼" pieces.

2. Combine the sour cream and mayonnaise until well blended.

3. Combine beans, corn, red pepper, habanero pepper, onion, and celery in a large mixing bowl. Stir in dressing until well coated.

4. Cover and refrigerate overnight. Serve chilled.

Serve on a bed of lettuce with a cold meat and cheese tray for a complete summertime meal.

Broccoli Salad v

What You Need

4 cups broccoli florets

1 medium yellow onion

1 cup yellow raisins

1 cup dry cooking sherry

½ cup lime juice

1 tablespoon dried cilantro

½ cup olive oil

1 teaspoon salt

1 teaspoon ground white pepper

1 cup canned mandarin oranges

½ cup blanched almond slivers

What You Do

1. Wash broccoli florets and cut into bite-sized pieces. Remove skin from onion and cut into ¼" pieces. Place raisins in 1 cup cooking sherry and let soak for 15 minutes.

2. Combine lime juice, cilantro, olive oil, salt and white pepper, and juice from the mandarin oranges. Mix well.

3. Combine broccoli, onion, raisins, mandarin oranges, and blanched almond slivers. Mix until well blended.

4. Pour dressing on top of broccoli mixture and stir until well blended.

5. Refrigerate for at least 1 hour before serving.

LEVEL **E**

SERVINGS **6**

Canned cactus strips are available at most large grocery stores today, although you can substitute another vegetable such as broccoli or cauliflower.

Cactus Salad v

What You Need

2 large red tomatoes

4 medium red radishes

2 cups drained canned cactus strips

½ cup sliced canned black olives

2 tablespoons ground coriander

¼ cup olive oil

¼ cup red wine vinegar

1 teaspoon garlic salt

1 teaspoon ground white pepper

½ teaspoon cayenne pepper

What You Do

1. Cut tomatoes into 1" pieces. Remove stems and roots from radishes and cut into ½" pieces. Combine these ingredients with cactus strips, olives, and coriander in a large mixing bowl.

2. In a small, covered container, mix the olive oil, red wine vinegar, garlic salt, white pepper, and cayenne pepper. Shake well to mix.

3. Pour dressing over the cactus strip mixture and toss until well mixed.

4. Chill before serving.

What's Coriander?

Coriander is a seed that comes either whole or ground. It is considered an aromatic spice because it gives off a wonderful smell, in addition to its strong flavor. It is especially good when the whole seeds are slightly roasted in a small frying pan before being added to a dish.

This is an excellent substitute for the vegetable course in any spicy meal.

Spinach Salad v

What You Need

1 large bunch of spinach

1 large red onion

4 medium red radishes

2 serrano chilies

½ cup goat cheese

½ cup pepitas (dried, hulled pumpkin seeds)

½ cup olive oil

¼ cup dry white wine

3 tablespoons lime juice

1 tablespoon Tabasco sauce

What You Do

1. Remove stems from spinach and wash leaves well. Dry on paper towels.

2. Remove skin from onion and cut into ¼" rounds. Remove stems and roots from radishes and cut into ¼" rounds. Remove stems and seeds from chilies and cut into ½" pieces. Crumble goat cheese.

3. Combine spinach, onion, pepitas, radishes, and chilies in a large mixing bowl.

4. In a small, covered container, combine the olive oil, white wine, lime juice, and Tabasco sauce. Shake until well blended.

5. Pour dressing over salad and toss until well coated. Top with crumbled goat cheese.

Veggies with Hot Pepper Dressing v

What You Need

1 cup fresh green beans

1 carrot

4 radishes

2 large red tomatoes

2 fresh or canned serrano peppers

1 cup red wine

1 cup olive oil

1 teaspoon garlic salt

½ teaspoon dried oregano

½ teaspoon cayenne pepper

1 cup broccoli florets

1 cup cauliflower florets

½ cup chopped green olives with pimientos

1 15-ounce canned corn, drained

What You Do

1. Cut ends off green beans then cut beans in half. Peel carrot and cut into ¼" rounds. Cut roots and stems from radishes and cut radishes into ¼" rounds. Cut tomatoes into 16 wedges each.

2. Mix these ingredients in a large mixing bowl.

3. Remove stems (but not seeds) from peppers and cut into ¼" pieces. Add to red wine and olive oil. Add garlic salt, oregano, and cayenne pepper. Place in a small, covered container and shake until well mixed.

4. Pour dressing over ingredients. Toss gently until well mixed.

5. Chill before serving for best results.

What Happened to the Salad?

Mexicans typically don't serve a salad course with their meals. If a green salad is served, it typically takes the place of the vegetable. As a result, many of their salads feature a wide variety of vegetables.

Carrot Chili Pepper Salad v

Serve with Empanaditas de Carne (see page 310).

What You Need

1 large carrot

2 celery ribs

3 green onions or scallions

1 fresh jalapeño pepper

1 cup canned pineapple chunks

1 cup mayonnaise

What You Do

1. Grate carrot. Cut celery into ¼" pieces. Remove roots from green onions or scallions and chop into ¼" pieces, including the green tops. Remove stem and seeds from jalapeño pepper and cut into ¼" pieces.

2. Combine carrot, celery, green onions, jalapeño pepper, and pineapple in a medium mixing bowl. Stir until well mixed.

3. Add 1 cup mayonnaise. Stir until all ingredients are covered.

Zesty Cheese Salad ᵥ

Serve with Grilled
Swordfish (see page
164).

What You Need

⅔ cup fresh cilantro
leaves

1 medium red onion

2 small poblano peppers

1 large avocado

1 medium jicama

1 pound shredded
mozzarella cheese

1 teaspoon garlic paste

1 teaspoon ground cumin

½ teaspoon fresh
oregano (or ¼ teaspoon
dry)

⅔ cup olive oil

½ teaspoon salt

½ teaspoon ground
black pepper

½ cup lime juice

What You Do

1. Remove stems from cilantro and chop leaves
   into ¼" pieces. Peel onion and cut into ¼" pieces.
   Remove stem and seeds from peppers and cut into
   ¼" pieces. Peel avocado and remove pit. Slice into
   2" lengths about ¼" thick. Peel jicama and cut into
   pieces about the size of match sticks.

2. In a large mixing bowl, combine onion, poblanos,
   avocado, jicama, and mozzarella cheese. Toss until
   well mixed.

3. In a medium covered container, combine the garlic
   paste, cumin, oregano, olive oil, salt, black pepper,
   and lime juice. Shake until well mixed. Pour dressing over the vegetables and cheese. Toss lightly.

How Do I Substitute Dry Spices?

Because dry spices have the water taken out of them, you usually substitute half the amount of dry for the fresh variety. However, many spices
lose their flavor when dried so it's best to use what the recipe calls for
if at all possible.

LEVEL **E**

SERVINGS **6**

Serve as a salad with Barbecued Pork Ribs (see page 119).

Mexican Coleslaw v

What You Need

3 tablespoons salad oil

½ cup cider vinegar

2 tablespoons white sugar

1½ teaspoons salt

1 teaspoon paprika

½ teaspoon dried mustard

1 teaspoon celery seed

1 green bell pepper

1 small yellow onion

¼ cup canned diced pimientos

1 (16-ounce) package shredded cabbage or coleslaw mix

½ cup sliced black olives

What You Do

1. In a small covered container, combine salad oil, cider vinegar, white sugar, salt, paprika, dried mustard, and celery seed. Cover and shake until well mixed.

2. Remove seeds and stem from green bell pepper and cut into ¼" pieces. Peel onion and cut into ¼" pieces. Dice pimientos if necessary.

3. In a large serving bowl, combine cabbage, bell pepper, pimientos, onion, and black olives. Toss gently until well mixed.

4. Pour dressing on top. Toss gently until well covered. Cover and refrigerate at least 1 hour before serving.

How Should I Clean Root Vegetables?

Clean root vegetables thoroughly by scrubbing them with a nail brush or scouring pad designated for that purpose. Because they grow in fertilized soil, they can harbor bacteria on their skins.

Carrot Salad v

LEVEL E
SERVINGS 4

This makes an excellent first course to Southwestern Fried Chicken (see page 154).

What You Need

6 large, fresh carrots

½ cup golden raisins

¾ cup orange juice

1 teaspoon sugar

⅛ teaspoon salt

¼ cup pistachio meats

What You Do

Peel carrots and grate. Combine carrots, raisins, orange juice, sugar, and salt in a medium-sized bowl. Cover and refrigerate 3–4 hours before serving. Right before serving, mix in pistachio meats.

Pineapple Coconut Salad v

LEVEL E
SERVINGS 6

For a tropical change of pace, add 1 cup mango or fresh papaya to this salad.

What You Need

2 cups canned chunk pineapple, drained

2 cups shredded coconut

2 cups shredded cabbage or coleslaw mix

1 cup mayonnaise

1 teaspoon lemon juice

6 large lettuce leaves

What You Do

Combine pineapple, coconut, cabbage, mayonnaise, and lemon juice in a large serving bowl. Toss gently until well mixed. Cover and chill for at least 1 hour before serving. Serve by scooping onto lettuce leaves.

This makes an excellent accompaniment to any beef dish.

Peppery Mango Salad v

What You Need

10 ripe mangoes

2 large Vidalia onions

8 fresh jalapeño peppers

½ cup vegetable oil

1½ cups cider vinegar

½ teaspoon salt

½ teaspoon ground white pepper

½ teaspoon white sugar

What You Do

1. Peel mangoes and slice fruit into ½" thick slices. Peel onion and cut into ¼" rounds. Remove stem and seeds from jalapeño peppers and cut into ¼" rounds. Combine these ingredients in a large mixing bowl.

2. Stir the oil, cider vinegar, salt, pepper, and sugar together. Pour over fruit, onion, and pepper mixture. Toss gently until mangoes, onions, and peppers are covered with dressing.

3. Refrigerate at least 2 hours before serving.

This makes an excellent counterpart to a heavy meat dish such as Caldo de Rez (see page 71).

Spicy Pineapple Salad v

What You Need

2 cups canned chunk pineapple with juice

1 medium red onion

1 bunch fresh cilantro

1 jalapeño pepper

½ teaspoon garlic powder

½ teaspoon oregano

½ teaspoon cayenne pepper

What You Do

1. Reserve pineapple juice. Peel onion and cut into ¼" rings. Remove stems from cilantro and roughly chop leaves into ½" pieces. Remove stem and seeds from jalapeño pepper and cut into ¼" rings.

2. Combine all ingredients in a medium serving bowl. Mix well.

3. Cover and chill in the refrigerator for at least 4 hours before serving.

Use this as a side
dish to complement
a spicy fish or
poultry meal.

Mexican Potato Salad   v

What You Need

1 pound small red potatoes

1 quart water

1 large tomato

¼ cup chopped green onions

¼ cup tomato salsa (see Tomato Salsa, page 12)

1 tablespoon olive oil

2 tablespoons lime juice

½ teaspoon salt

½ teaspoon ground black pepper

½ cup sliced ripe olives

1 tablespoon fresh cilantro

What You Do

1. Clean and quarter potatoes. Boil in 1 quart water until tender but not mushy. (They may also be cooked in the microwave.) Drain and set aside.

2. Cut tomato into ½" pieces.

3. Combine all ingredients except potatoes and tomatoes and cook uncovered on low heat for 5 minutes.

4. Pour sauce over potatoes, add tomatoes, and store in a covered bowl in the refrigerator for 8–12 hours before serving.

What are the Different Types of Potatoes?

Most of us eat a great deal of potatoes but are we aware of how many different types there are? New potatoes are usually very small brown potatoes that have a sweet flavor. Red potatoes can be either new or larger and have a mild flavor. Bakers are large, tough potatoes. New varieties such as golden-fleshed and purple-fleshed potatoes offer other tastes.

Chicken-Stuffed Avocado

What You Need

2 medium avocados

¼ cup fresh lime juice

1 cup cooked chicken breast

2 medium tomatoes

4 scallions or green onions

1 cup lettuce

12 green olives stuffed with pimientos

½ teaspoon salt

1 teaspoon black pepper

2 tablespoons red wine vinegar

½ cup shredded Cheddar cheese

What You Do

1. Peel avocados. Slice in half and remove pits. Sprinkle with lime juice.

2. Remove skin from the chicken and chop into ½" pieces.

3. Chop tomatoes into ¼" pieces. Remove skin from scallions/onions and chop into ¼" pieces. Tear lettuce into ½" pieces. Cut olives into quarters.

4. Combine all ingredients except avocados and cheese in a medium-sized bowl.

5. Place ¼ of the mixture into each avocado half. Sprinkle cheese on top.

LEVEL **H**

SERVINGS **4**

Serve atop a bed of lettuce with fresh Tostadas (see page 287).

Mussel Ceviche

What You Need

1 pound fresh shelled mussels

½ cup lime juice

1 small Vidalia onion

2 habanero peppers

½ cup chopped canned tomatillos with juice

½ cup tomato juice

½ cup clam juice

1 teaspoon salt

3 Key limes

What You Do

1. Combine the mussels and lime juice in a small glass or ceramic container. Cover and refrigerate for 1 hour.

2. Remove skin from onion and cut into ¼" pieces. Remove stem and seeds from habanero peppers and cut into ¼" pieces.

3. Drain lime juice and put mussels in a medium-sized mixing bowl. Add the onions, chilies, tomatillos with their juice, tomato juice, clam juice, salt, and fresh-squeezed juice from 3 Key limes. Stir well. Refrigerate in a glass or ceramic container for 4–12 hours.

Can I Substitute Canned or Frozen Mussels for Fresh?

Fresh mussels will not smell fishy. The water they sit in will be clear and the shells will be bright, not filmy. Frozen and canned mussels simply don't have the same flavor as the fresh ones. However, some people substitute canned oysters for fresh mussels and consider it a good tradeoff.

Caribbean Coast Pickled Tuna

This makes an excellent summer luncheon when served with Fruit Compote (see page 241).

What You Need

1 pound fresh tuna steak

¼ cup lime juice

1 medium yellow onion

1 garlic clove

2 canned jalapeño peppers

¼ cup vegetable oil

½ teaspoon oregano

½ teaspoon cumin

¾ cup wine vinegar

½ cup sliced pimiento-stuffed olives

What You Do

1. Put tuna in a medium stock pot. Add ½" of water. Cover and heat on low until fish is cooked through. Fish should flake easily with a fork. When cool, flake fish and put in a small bowl.

2. Add lime juice over fish and let stand about 10 minutes (while preparing the rest of the meal).

3. Peel onion and slice into ⅛"-thick rounds. Peel garlic and mince. Cut jalapeño peppers into thin strips.

4. Heat oil in a medium frying pan to medium temperature. Add onion, chilies, and garlic. Cook about 5 minutes, until onion is limp but not brown. Stir in oregano and cumin. Stir in vinegar. Bring to a boil.

5. Pour sauce over fish and stir until well coated.

6. Cover and refrigerate at least 8 hours before serving. Garnish with olive slices.

Chapter 5
Beef and Pork

Shredded Beef

Shredded beef can be used in enchiladas, tacos, and many other dishes that call for either beef chunks or ground beef.

For less bite, add the jalapeños to the pot whole.

This is a great slow-cooker recipe.

What You Need

1 bunch fresh cilantro

⅓ cup canned sliced (or 3 fresh) jalapeño peppers

4 pounds top sirloin

1 teaspoon garlic paste

1 bay leaf

1 (14½-ounce) can diced tomatoes

1 teaspoon salt

2 teaspoons ground black pepper

1 (8-ounce) bottle Italian salad dressing

What You Do

1. Remove stems from cilantro. Remove stems and seeds from jalapeño peppers.

2. Place all ingredients in a heavy pot. Cover and cook over medium heat for about 5 hours.

3. Remove meat from broth, cool, and shred with forks or in a food processor. Discard broth.

?

How Do I Choose a Bell Pepper?

Bell peppers have different flavors depending on their color. Green is the most acidic and sour tasting. Red has the most peppery flavor. Yellow and orange have a gentle flavor. Combine them to create unique flavors and a beautiful dish.

Mexican Pot Roast

Thicken the sauce by adding ¼ cup flour and cooking it on the stove until it becomes a gravy.

Serve drizzled over the meat or over mashed potatoes.

What You Need

3 tablespoons olive oil

½ cup flour

3-pound pot roast

1 large yellow onion

1 (14½-ounce) can diced tomatoes

¼ teaspoon oregano

4 morita chilies

1 teaspoon salt

½ teaspoon garlic paste

What You Do

1. Preheat oven to 350°F.

2. Pour olive oil into a large skillet and turn heat to medium. Dredge flour into beef by pounding it in until no more flour will stick. Place beef in the skillet. Cook, turning until the meat is brown on all sides.

3. Peel onion. Cut onion into ¼"-thick rings.

4. Place pot roast in a roasting pan. Cover with remaining ingredients.

5. Cook covered for 2 hours.

What's a Morita Chili Pepper?

Morita chilies are a type of jalapeño that has been dried and smoked. They tend to be a bit hotter than regular jalapeños and less smoky than chipotles.

Citrus Veal

Serve this with a fresh fruit salad to carry through the fruity flavor of the dish.

What You Need

4 veal cutlets

¼ teaspoon cinnamon

¼ teaspoon cloves

1 teaspoon salt

1 large white onion

2 garlic cloves

2 oranges

1 tablespoon vegetable oil

1 cup orange juice

¼ cup lime juice

What You Do

1. Preheat oven to 350°F.

2. Season both sides of veal cutlets with cinnamon, cloves, and salt.

3. Remove skin from onion and cut into 1" pieces. Remove skin from garlic and cut thinly. Cut oranges into ¼" rounds with rind remaining on the oranges.

4. Pour oil in the bottom of a medium baking dish. Place veal cutlets in the dish so they don't overlap. Pour the orange juice and lime juice on the top. Place the onions, oranges, and garlic on top.

5. Cover baking dish. Place in oven and cook for 1 hour.

How Do I Choose a Good Veal?

Veal is obtained from a young cow, often a male dairy cow. The veal calves are fed a special diet of milk-based products and are encouraged not to get a great deal of exercise. As a result, the meat is very tender and pale. A good veal steak will be nearly as white and texture-less as chicken breasts. It should have less than a half inch of fat around the edges.

This can be used as a dip, as a filling for tacos, or as a side dish.

Salpicon

What You Need

3 cups shredded beef (see Shredded Beef, page 102)

1 (8-ounce) bottle Italian salad dressing

2 avocados

1 cup cooked or canned garbanzo beans, drained

½ pound shredded Monterey jack cheese

1 cup canned jalapeño peppers, drained

1 bunch parsley

What You Do

1. Arrange beef in a 9" × 11" casserole.

2. Cover with salad dressing. Cover and marinate in refrigerator overnight.

3. Preheat oven to 300°F. Remove skin and nut from avocados and cut into ½" slices.

4. Spread layers over the beef in this order: garbanzo beans, cheese, jalapeño peppers, avocados, parsley. Place in oven for 20 minutes.

Serve with
Pineapple Coconut
Salad
(see page 94).

Fideo con Carne

What You Need

¼ cabbage

¼ cup vegetable oil

18-ounce vermicelli noodles

¾ teaspoon garlic paste

1 pound lean ground beef

¼ teaspoon ground black pepper

⅔ cup canned diced tomatoes

¼ teaspoon cumin

¼ teaspoon salt

2 quarts water

What You Do

1. Chop cabbage into 1" pieces.

2. Bring oil to medium temperature in a large frying pan. Add vermicelli noodles. Cook until noodles are lightly browned. Remove noodles and set aside.

3. In same pan, add garlic paste and ground beef. Cook until beef is browned. Drain oil.

4. Add vermicelli, ground pepper, tomatoes, cumin, and salt. Stir until all ingredients are mixed. Add water. Bring to a simmer, cover, and cook for 10 minutes.

5. Add cabbage. Stir and simmer uncovered for 15 minutes.

This goes very well with Easy Huevos Rancheros (see page 129), or any other egg dish.

Chorizo (Mexican Sausage)

What You Need

2 pounds ground pork

2 tablespoons paprika

1 teaspoon ground black pepper

1 teaspoon ground oregano

1 teaspoon ground cumin

¼ teaspoon ground coriander seeds

⅔ cup vinegar

1 teaspoon garlic powder

2 tablespoons salt

2 tablespoons cayenne pepper

What You Do

1. Place all ingredients in a large mixing bowl. Mix with your hands until all ingredients are well blended.

2. Place in an airtight container. Refrigerate for at least 2 days.

3. Form into patties for frying.

How is Sausage Made?

Virtually every culture that slaughters animals has invented some type of sausage. Traditionally it is made with the little pieces of meat that are left over from the slaughter—ears, nose, and so on. Spices are added for both flavor and preservation. Many cultures, including the Mexicans, force the meat mixture into cleaned-out intestines to make links.

Mexican Meat Loaf

Serve with
Pineapple Coconut
Salad
(see page 94).

What You Need

2 hardboiled eggs

1 raw egg

1 pound ground beef

½ pound ground pork

½ cup chopped onion

⅔ cup uncooked oats

1 teaspoon salt

¼ teaspoon black pepper

1 cup Red Chili Sauce
(see page 17)

¼ cup sliced pimiento-
stuffed green olives

What You Do

1. Preheat oven to 350°F.

2. Peel hardboiled eggs and slice into ¼" rounds. Beat raw egg until whites and yolk are well mixed.

3. Combine ground beef, ground pork, onion, oats, beaten egg, salt, pepper, and ½ cup of Red Chili Sauce. Mix with your hands until well blended.

4. Pack half of the meat mixture into an 8" × 4" × 2" loaf pan. Arrange hard-cooked eggs in a row down the center of the loaf. Arrange olive slices on either side of eggs. Press eggs and olives slightly into meat mixture. Cover with remaining half of meat mixture. Pour remaining ½ cup of Red Chili Sauce on top. Bake for 1 hour.

What Makes a Pepper Hot?

The heat of a chili pepper is caused by the presence of a volatile oil called capsaicin, which can burn the skin and eyes. As a result, if you are handling a lot of chilies, such as picking them fresh from your garden, it's important to wear rubber gloves. Always wash your hands after handling even a small amount of chili pepper.

Serve with Eggplant
Casserole (see
page 197), and
Pistachio Coconut
Flan (see page 268).

Albondigas (Meatballs)

What You Need

4 canned chipotle peppers

1 cup chopped onion

¼ cup vegetable oil

1 cup canned tomato
sauce

¼ teaspoon garlic paste

2 cups canned or fresh
beef broth

2½ teaspoons salt

½ teaspoon dried oregano

½ teaspoon cumin

2 slices dry bread

¼ cup milk

1 pound ground beef

½ pound ground pork

¼ pound ground
cooked ham

1 egg

¼ teaspoon ground
black pepper

What You Do

1. Chop chipotle peppers into ¼" pieces.

2. Put ¼ cup vegetable oil in a large frying pan and heat
   to medium. Cook ½ cup onion in oil until onions are
   clear and tender. Add tomato sauce, garlic paste,
   beef broth, 1 teaspoon salt, oregano, cumin, and
   half the chipotle peppers. Heat to boiling, stirring
   constantly. Reduce heat and let simmer.

3. Crumble bread into ½" pieces or smaller. Put bread
   chunks and milk into a small bowl and mix well.

4. Combine beef, pork, ham, and remaining onion. Mix
   with your hands until well blended.

5. Beat egg slightly and add 1½ teaspoons salt, black
   pepper, and remainder of chopped chilies. Add egg
   mixture and bread/milk mixture to meat. Mix until
   well blended. Form into balls about 1½" in diameter. Put meatballs into simmering sauce, cover, and
   simmer 1 hour.

White Chili

Top this chili with
Monterey jack
cheese, crushed
tortilla chips, and
a dollop of sour
cream.

What You Need

1 pound dry navy beans

12 cups chicken broth (see Chicken Stock, page 124)

½ teaspooon garlic paste

½ cup chopped onion

2 (4-ounce) cans green chilies

2 teaspoons ground cumin

1½ teaspoon dried oregano

½ teaspoon ground cloves

¼ teaspoon cayenne pepper

4 cups diced cooked chicken, light and dark meat

What You Do

1. Soak beans in 4 cups water for 2–10 hours. Or use Quick & Easy Beans (see page 210) process to prepare for cooking.

2. Place chicken broth in large pot on low heat. Add beans.

3. Add remaining ingredients to the pot. Stir well.

6. Simmer for 3 hours.

Pork & Potatoes

Serve with Pineapple Coconut Salad (see page 94), for a blend of sweet and spicy.

What You Need

3 large white onions

10 assorted whole chili peppers

5 medium-sized new potatoes

1 (3-pound) pork roast

1 teaspoon garlic paste

10 whole cloves

1 cinnamon stick

10 black peppercorns

1 teaspoon whole cumin seeds

2 tablespoons white vinegar

What You Do

1. Preheat oven to 350°F.

2. Peel the onions and cut into quarters. Remove the stems from the chili peppers and cut in half lengthwise (do not remove the seeds). Peel the potatoes and cut in half.

3. Place the pork in a large baking pan. Cover with onions, garlic paste, chili peppers, cloves, cinnamon stick, peppercorns, and cumin seeds. Add just enough water to cover the ingredients. Cover and cook for 1 hour.

4. Stir the mixture. Add the potatoes, cover, and cook for 1 hour or until the potatoes are soft. Ten minutes before serving, remove the spices and add vinegar. Leave uncovered for the last 10 minutes.

Can I Fix Mushy Potatoes?

Have your raw potatoes gone mushy? They're still good if you use them right away. Remove the peels and slice the potatoes thickly. Put them in a soup or stew and no one will know they were past their prime.

Substitute meats and cheeses.

Add onions or olive slices.

Lonches

What You Need

½ pound Monterey jack cheese

6 slices bacon

6 large hard rolls

1½ cups Red Chili Sauce (see page 17)

What You Do

1. Heat oven to 350°F. Slice cheese thinly. Fry bacon until crisp. Drain grease.

2. Split rolls in half horizontally but not quite all the way through. Fill generously with cheese and top with a bacon strip. Close rolls to form sandwiches and place on a cookie sheet.

3. Put in oven for 5 to 10 minutes or until rolls are hot and cheese is melted.

4. While rolls are baking, heat sauce to bubbling.

5. Place each filled roll in a soup bowl and ladle ¼ cup sauce over the top.

LEVEL **E**

SERVINGS **8**

Serve with Mexican Hot Chocolate (see page 302), on the next cool day.

Taco Soup

What You Need

½ cup chopped onion

⅔ cup chopped green bell pepper

2 pounds lean ground beef

1 tablespoon paprika

1 tablespoon chili powder

1 tablespoon salt

1 tablespoon ground black pepper

3 14½-ounce cans diced tomatoes

2 15-ounce cans pinto beans

1 15-ounce can kidney beans

1 15-ounce can golden hominy

1 15-ounce can whole kernel corn

6 cups water

4 Tostadas (see page 287)

What You Do

1. Peel onion and chop into ¼" pieces. Remove stem and seeds from green bell pepper and chop into ¼" pieces.

2. Put ground beef, onion, green pepper, paprika, chili powder, salt, and ground black pepper in a frying pan on medium heat. Cook until ground beef is browned.

3. Add ground beef mixture to a large stock pot. Add canned stewed tomatoes with juice; pinto beans with juice; kidney beans with juice; hominy with juice; and whole kernel corn with juice.

4. Stir and add 6 cups of water. Bring to a boil. Turn temperature to medium-low. Cover and simmer for 2 hours. Top with crumbled tostadas before serving.

What's Hominy?

Hominy is actually dried white field corn that has been cooked with powdered lime until its skin falls off. The kernel's eye is taken out, and the kernel opens up until it resembles a piece of wet popcorn.

Texas Chili

Serve with Jalapeño
Corn Bread (see
page 184).

What You Need

2 pounds lean ground beef

¾ teaspoon garlic paste

1 cup chopped onion

2 cups canned diced tomatoes, with juice

3 cups canned tomato sauce

1 tablespoon salt

½ teaspoon ground black pepper

3 teaspoons chili powder

1 teaspoon oregano

3 tablespoons sugar

4 cups canned kidney beans

What You Do

1. In a large skillet on medium heat, cook ground beef until it is browned. Drain grease.

2. Put all ingredients in a large pot and simmer on medium heat until heated through.

LEVEL **E**

SERVINGS **6**

Add a side of Extra Special Frijoles Refritos (see page 221).

Taco Skillet Casserole

What You Need

8 corn tortillas (see Basic Corn Tortillas, page 285)

1½ pounds ground beef

¼ cup chopped onion

¼ teaspoon garlic paste

1 teaspoon salt

½ teaspoon black pepper

1 teaspoon chili powder

2 cups canned tomato sauce

½ cup vegetable oil

½ cup shredded Cheddar cheese

½ cup shredded lettuce

What You Do

1. Cut tortillas into ½" wide strips.

2. Crumble ground beef into a large frying pan and brown on medium heat. Pour off excess fat. Add onion and garlic and cook about 5 minutes longer, until onion is soft. Stir frequently. Stir in salt, pepper, chili powder, and tomato sauce and continue cooking over low heat about 15 minutes longer. Stir frequently.

3. In a separate frying pan, heat ½ cup vegetable oil to medium-high. Fry tortilla strips until crisp. Drain on absorbent paper.

4. Stir tortilla strips into meat mixture and cook about 5 minutes longer, stirring frequently. Sprinkle with cheese. As soon as cheese melts, remove from heat. Top with shredded lettuce and serve immediately.

Can Corn Husks Be Used as a Spice?

The Mexican culture is unique in using corn husks to spice its food. Most often used in corn tamales, the husks are also used as a wrapper for other foods such as candy. When leaving the husk on for cooking the corn, you will notice a distinctly earthy taste that is transferred to the food.

This is just as traditional if made with beef, but it never contains tomatoes.

Northern Border Chili con Carne

What You Need

1 pound cubed pork steak

1 pound cubed veal steak

2 tablespoons olive oil

1 medium yellow onion

2 garlic cloves

1 teaspoon dried oregano

1 teaspoon salt

2 cups canned kidney beans

6 jalapeño peppers

What You Do:

1. Place meat in a large frying pan along with the olive oil. Cook on medium heat until the meat is lightly browned on all sides.

2. Remove skin from onion and garlic. Remove stem and seeds from peppers. Cut onion into quarters. Place peppers, onion, garlic, oregano, and salt in blender or food processor and blend on medium setting until you have a purée. Add purée to meat. Stir and cook uncovered for 10 minutes.

3. Add kidney beans to frying pan. Reduce heat, cover, and cook for 1 to 2 hours.

Do Mexicans Spice Their Ground Beef?

Many Americans believe that Mexicans spiced their ground beef with hot peppers to avoid tasting the decay that was obviously present given the hot weather and no refrigeration. The truth is that Mexicans rarely eat ground beef. Most of their beef, pork, and veal dishes use steak that traditionally was cut from freshly slaughtered animals.

Tostadas from Guadalajara

These make a wonderful replacement for a salad or they can be a light lunch all by themselves.

You also can make petite tostadas and use these as appetizers.

What You Need

1 tablespoon olive oil

2 tablespoons vinegar

1 teaspoon salt

½ teaspoon ground white pepper

1 cup shredded lettuce

4 spicy sausage patties

2 cups Refried Beans (see page 211)

1 medium yellow onion

8 freshly made (still warm) Tostadas (see page 287)

2 cups Guacamole (see page 16)

1¾ cup shredded mozzarella cheese

What You Do

1. Combine olive oil, vinegar, salt, and white pepper in a small covered container Shake until well mixed, then pour over the lettuce and set aside.

2. Crumble the sausage patties and heat on medium in a small frying pan. Cook until browned. Heat beans in a small saucepan.

3. Peel onion and chop into ¼" pieces. Drain lettuce.

4. Put the ingredients in layers on the Tostadas in the following order: Refried Beans, sausage, onion, Guacamole, lettuce, cheese.

Pork Roast with Apples

Serve with Turnip & Mustard Leaf Rolls (see page 203), for a unique combination of flavors.

What You Need

1 (3-pound) pork roast

½ teaspoon oregano

½ teaspoon thyme

½ teaspoon coriander

1 teaspoon salt

1 teaspoon black pepper

2 tablespoons vegetable oil

3 medium green apples (such as Granny Smith)

1 cup apple juice

1 teaspoon garlic paste

½ cup chopped onion

1 cup water

1 (¼-ounce) envelope unflavored gelatin

½ cup dry white wine

What You Do

1. Preheat oven to 350°F

2. Season pork roast with the oregano, thyme, coriander, salt, and black pepper.

3. Place 2 tablespoons vegetable oil in a large frying pan. Add pork roast. Cook on medium heat, turning the pork roast until all sides are browned.

4. Remove stem and core from 2 apples and slice into ½" slices. Put pork roast in a large baking dish. Cover with apple juice mixed with garlic paste. Sprinkle apple pieces and onion. Cover and bake for 1 hour.

5. Remove peel, stem, and core from remaining apple. Place in food processor or blender and blend until puréed.

6. Boil 1 cup water. Add gelatin. Stir in wine and apple purée. Cool in refrigerator for 15 minutes.

7. Remove meat from oven. Cut into ½" pieces and arrange on a platter. Top with gelatin mixture right before serving.

Serve with Grilled Corn on the Cob (see page 192).

Barbecued Pork Ribs

What You Need

12 garlic cloves

1 small red onion

8 chipotle peppers

½ cup water

¼ cup red wine vinegar

1 tablespoon dried oregano

1 cup honey

½ cup Dijon mustard

1 teaspoon salt

1 teaspoon ground black pepper

4 pounds pork ribs

What You Do

1. Preheat grill to medium setting.

2. Peel garlic and chop finely. Peel onion and cut into ¼" pieces.

3. Remove stems from chipotle peppers. Put ½ cup water in a small saucepan and add peppers. Cover and simmer on low setting for 10 minutes or until peppers are plump. Drain water. Remove peppers and cut into ¼" pieces.

4. Combine all ingredients (except ribs) in a medium saucepan. Stir well. Bring mixture to a boil. Cover and simmer for 10 minutes.

5. Use as a basting sauce while grilling ribs. Reserve ½ cup to be served as a dipping sauce with the meal.

What's the Best Way to Cook Ribs?

Ribs must be cooked very slowly to ensure that they get done. Too hot a temperature and the meat will burn off. Some people boil the ribs in beer or water for 10 minutes before grilling to ensure the meat doesn't dry out.

Pork with Pineapple

Serve with Red Rice
(see page 212).

What You Need

3 pounds pork loin

1 large fresh red tomato

1 tablespoon vegetable oil

½ cup chopped onion

2 cups canned pineapple chunks with juice

1 cup canned beef stock or bouillon

¼ cup dry sherry

⅓ cup sliced pimientos

½ teaspoon chili powder

1 teaspoon salt

½ teaspoon black pepper

2 tablespoons flour

What You Do

1. Cut meat into 2" chunks. Remove stem from tomato and chop into ¼" pieces.

2. Heat vegetable oil in a large frying pan. Add meat and brown well on all sides. Add onion and cook about 5 minutes, or until soft.

3. Add pineapple with juice, beef stock, sherry, pimiento, tomato, and chili powder to the skillet. Stir until well mixed. Bring to a boil, reduce heat to simmering, and add salt and pepper.

4. Cover and simmer until meat is tender, about 1½ hours. Stir occasionally.

5. Just before serving, sprinkle flour over simmering sauce and stir in. Cook and stir until sauce is thickened.

This makes a unique breakfast dish when served with fresh fruit.

Baked Noodles with Chorizo

What You Need

¼ pound chorizo sausage or any hot, spicy sausage

4 tablespoons vegetable oil

1 (7-ounce) package small egg noodles

½ cup chopped onion

2 cups chicken broth (see Chicken Stock, page 124)

1 cup cottage cheese

1 cup sour cream

1 teaspoon Tabasco or other hot sauce

1 teaspoon salt

½ teaspoon ground black pepper

½ cup shredded Parmesan cheese

What You Do

1. Preheat oven to 350°F.

2. Fry sausage in a large frying pan until cooked through. Crumble sausage as it fries. Remove meat from frying pan and set aside.

3. Add oil to frying pan until about 1" deep. Stir in uncooked noodles and onion. Fry until noodles are lightly browned and onion is soft. Stir often to prevent burning.

4. Return chorizo to frying pan. Stir in broth.

5. Transfer to an ovenproof casserole. Bake about 15 minutes or until all liquid is absorbed by noodles.

6. Remove from oven. Stir in cottage cheese and sour cream. Add hot sauce, salt, and pepper. Sprinkle Parmesan cheese on top. Return to oven and bake about 10 minutes or until bubbling hot.

Serve as a stew over white rice or use as a filling for enchiladas.

Pork Picadillo

What You Need

1½ pounds pork roast

¼ cup vegetable oil

½ cup chopped onion

1 cup Green Chili Sauce (see page 18)

1 cup frozen or canned peas, thawed or drained

1 cup frozen or canned carrots, thawed or drained

½ cup chicken broth (see Chicken Stock, page 124)

½ teaspoon garlic paste

1 teaspoon salt

¼ teaspoon ground black pepper

¼ teaspoon dried ginger

1 bay leaf, crumbled

¼ cup canned chopped jalapeños

What You Do

1. Put pork roast in a large stew pot and add just enough water to cover. Cook meat on medium temperature 1 to 3 hours or until tender. Shred the meat by pulling it apart into strips.

2. Heat vegetable oil on medium-high in a large frying pan. Add onions and cook until limp but not brown. Add all ingredients to frying pan. Stir well. Reduce heat to low. Cover and cook 30 minutes.

What Does *Picadillo* Mean?

Picadillo literally means "meat and vegetable hash." As a result, the variations are endless. Some versions call for vegetables while others call for fruits and nuts. Get creative and see if you can discover your own unique variation.

Chapter 6
Poultry and Eggs

Chicken Stock

What You Need

1 medium yellow onion

2 large carrots

2 celery ribs

2–3 pounds of chicken bones (leftovers are great)

1 teaspoon salt

1 teaspoon ground black pepper

1 tablespoon dried parsley

1 gallon water

What You Do

1. Remove skin from onion. Clean carrots and celery and cut in half.

2. Add all ingredients to a large stock pot. Bring to a boil. Reduce heat, cover, and let simmer for 4 hours.

3. Strain the broth, pick any meat from the bones, and discard the vegetables and bones.

LEVEL **E**

SERVINGS **⋆**

*This recipe yields 1 to 1½ pounds.

Spicy Chicken can be used in enchiladas, tacos, and many other dishes that call for either beef chunks or ground beef.

Use fresh jalapeño peppers whole for less of a bite.

This is another good slow cooker recipe.

Spicy Chicken

What You Need

1 bunch fresh cilantro

1 frying chicken (about 2½ pounds)

1 teaspoon garlic paste

1 bay leaf

1 (14½-ounce) can diced tomatoes

⅓ cup canned sliced (or 3 fresh) jalapeño peppers

1 teaspoon salt

2 teaspoons ground black pepper

1 (8-ounce) bottle Italian salad dressing

What You Do

1. Remove stems from cilantro.

2. Place all ingredients in a heavy pot. Cover and cook over medium heat for about 5 hours.

3. Remove meat from broth and cool. Remove meat from bones and shred meat with forks or in a food processor. Discard broth, skin, and bones.

This is a perfect meal for Sunday brunch, or it can be served as the main course in a vegetarian meal.

Chili Relleno Soufflé v

What You Need

4 eggs

1 cup evaporated milk

⅔ cups flour

1 pound shredded Cheddar cheese

1 pound shredded Monterey jack cheese

½ cup drained canned jalapeño peppers

1 (8-ounce) can tomato sauce

What You Do

1. Preheat oven to 350°F.

2. Mix eggs, milk, and flour.

3. Layer ⅓ of the cheese then ½ of the egg mixture and ½ of the peppers and tomato sauce into a rectangular baking pan. Repeat layers. Reserve final ⅓ of cheese.

4. Bake uncovered for 30–45 minutes. Cover with remaining cheese and bake for 15 minutes

What are Alternatives to Chicken Eggs?

While Americans typically only eat chicken eggs, other birds' eggs can provide some interesting taste sensations. Try duck or goose eggs when baking to give more fluffiness to your cakes and bars. They also have a sweeter taste in casseroles and even as scrambled eggs.

Spinach Egg Bake v

What You Need

1 (10-ounce) package chopped spinach

1 (8-ounce) package fresh mushrooms

1 small white onion

6 eggs

2 cups diced cooked ham

2 cups small curd cottage cheese

½ cup butter

6 tablespoons flour

1 (12-ounce) package shredded Cheddar cheese

¼ cup drained canned jalapeño peppers

What You Do

1. Preheat oven to 350°F.

2. Thaw spinach and squeeze out water. Slice mushrooms in thin slices. Remove skin from onion and chop into ¼" pieces.

3. Beat eggs until whites and yolks are well blended.

4. Mix all ingredients in a large mixing bowl. Stir well until all ingredients are blended.

5. Pour into a 9" × 13" baking dish. Bake for 1 hour. Let stand 10 minutes before cutting.

What are the Different Onion Varieties?

Onions vary in sweetness. Vidalia tend to be the sweetest, followed by red, then yellow. White onions are the least sweet and are better in meat dishes than in soups.

This is a perfect breakfast meal served with Mexican Coffee (see page 303).

Mexican Frittata v

What You Need

3 cups whole milk

1½ cups flour

½ teaspoon salt

6 eggs

1 tablespoon vegetable oil

1½ pounds fresh chili peppers, your choice

1½ pounds shredded medium Cheddar cheese

1½ pounds shredded Monterey jack cheese

1 avocado

1 red bell pepper

What You Do

1. Preheat oven to 375°F.

2. Blend milk, flour, salt, and eggs. Spread oil over bottom and sides of 9" × 13" pan. Remove stems and seeds from chili peppers and cut into 1" pieces. Mix cheeses.

3. Place half of peppers in a layer on the bottom of the pan. Top with half of the cheese. Add the rest of the peppers. Add the rest of the cheese. Pour the egg mixture over the top. Bake for 40 minutes.

4. Remove skin and pit from avocado and cut into slices. Remove seeds and stem from red pepper and cut into 1" pieces. Use avocado and red pepper as garnish.

?

How Can I Turn a Meat Dish into a Vegetarian Dish?

To turn any meat dish into an instant vegetarian entrée, substitute morel mushrooms for the meat. Be sure to substitute by volume, not weight, because even these heavier mushrooms weigh less than meat.

Easy Huevos Rancheros v

Serve with a side of Extra-Special Frijoles Refritos (see page 221).

What You Need

1 avocado

1 tablespoon vegetable oil

4 eggs

4 corn tortillas (see Basic Corn Tortillas, page 285)

1 cup tomato salsa (see Tomato Salsa, page 12)

What You Do

1. Peel avocado and remove pit. Slice fruit into ½"-thick slices.

2. Heat oil to medium temperature in a medium frying pan. Add eggs. Fry to your liking.

3. Remove eggs and put tortillas in the frying pan. Fry 30 seconds on each side. Place 1 egg on top of each flattened tortilla. Cover egg with salsa. Garnish with avocado slices.

Spice this dish up any way you like. Add hot peppers, oregano, or dill weed, for example.

Huevos Bogotano v

What You Need

½ pound ground sausage

½ pound fresh or frozen corn

12 eggs

¼ teaspoon onion powder

½ teaspoon salt

½ teaspoon ground black pepper

What You Do

1. Crumble sausage and cook over medium heat in a medium frying pan until cooked but not browned, stirring frequently. Remove sausage and spread on a paper towel to absorb excess fat. Wipe grease from frying pan with a paper towel.

2. Put corn in a small saucepan and heat at medium temperature until thoroughly warmed.

3. Crack eggs into a medium mixing bowl. Add onion powder, salt, and pepper. Beat until light and fluffy.

4. Pour eggs in the frying pan and stir in sausage and corn. Cook over low heat, stirring frequently, until the eggs are done.

?

How Do I Choose Fresh Eggs?

Fresh eggs will be translucent when held up to light. When you break the egg, the white should be clear and the yolk should be shiny. Yolks can vary in color, depending on the diet and breed of chicken the egg came from.

Serve with fresh cantaloupe and honeydew melon slices.

Eggs Chilaquiles v

What You Need

4 corn tortillas (see Basic Corn Tortillas, page 285)

2 medium red tomatoes

1 small white onion

4 eggs

2 tablespoons butter or margarine

½ teaspoon salt

¼ teaspoon ground black pepper

½ teaspoon Tabasco or other hot sauce

½ cup grated Parmesan cheese

What You Do

1. Cut tortillas into ½" strips. Remove stems from tomatoes and chop into ¼" pieces. Peel onion and chop into ¼" pieces. Lightly beat eggs.

2. Melt butter or margarine in a large skillet at medium-high heat. Fry tortilla strips in butter or margarine until golden brown.

3. Stir in tomatoes and onion and heat to boiling.

4. Stir in eggs, salt, pepper, and Tabasco sauce. Cook until eggs are set, stirring frequently.

5. Top with Parmesan cheese. Serve immediately.

Serve with Pastelitos
(see page 244).

Scrambled Egg Tacos   v

What You Need

1 teaspoon butter

½ cup tomato salsa (see Tomato Salsa, page 12)

8 eggs

⅓ cup cream

½ teaspoon salt

4 corn tortillas (see Basic Corn Tortillas, page 285)

½ cup shredded Monterey jack cheese

What You Do

1. Melt butter in a large frying pan. Add tomato salsa and heat.

2. Beat eggs with cream and salt. Pour egg mixture into hot salsa and cook over medium heat, stirring constantly, until eggs are set.

3. While eggs are cooking, heat tortillas in an ungreased medium-hot skillet or griddle, turning frequently.

4. Place a hot, soft tortilla on a plate and spoon eggs on top. Sprinkle with cheese. Serve immediately.

What Egg Substitutions Can I Make?

Egg yolks contain all of the fat and cholesterol in an egg. Use egg whites instead of whole eggs when making pasta, cakes, and other dishes. Usually two egg whites can be substituted for one whole egg.

Serve this with simple rice and vegetable dishes so you don't detract from the complex flavors in the chicken.

Jalapeño Chicken

What You Need

4 garlic cloves

4 fresh jalapeño peppers

1 cup orange juice

1 cup honey

¼ cup lime juice

1 teaspoon salt

1 teaspoon cayenne pepper

1 cut up fryer (2½–3½ pounds)

What You Do

1. Preheat oven to 350°F.

2. Remove skin from garlic. Remove stem and seeds from jalapeño peppers.

3. Put garlic, peppers, orange juice, honey, lime juice, salt, and cayenne pepper in a blender or food processor and blend on medium setting for 5 minutes, or until peppers and garlic are well chopped.

4. Place chicken in a roasting pan. Brush glaze on chicken liberally but save about half for later.

5. Cook for 1½ hours. After 30 minutes, turn chicken and again glaze liberally. After another 30 minutes, turn chicken over again and use remaining glaze.

Cinnamon Fried Chicken

If there is extra room in the roasting pan, wash potatoes, leaving the skin on and quarter them.

Place them in with the chicken to bake.

What You Need

4 skin-on chicken breasts

1 cup milk

1 cup flour

2 tablespoons cinnamon

1 teaspoon cayenne pepper

1 tablespoon salt

1 teaspoon nutmeg

1 teaspoon ground cloves

4 tablespoons vegetable oil

What You Do

1. Preheat oven to 300°F.

2. Wash chicken thoroughly. Pour milk into a soup bowl and dunk chicken breasts in milk until completely coated. Discard remaining milk.

3. In another soup bowl, mix the flour, cinnamon, cayenne pepper, salt, nutmeg, and cloves. Roll each breast in the flour mixture until well coated.

4. Put vegetable oil in a roasting pan. Place chicken breasts skin side down in the roasting pan and put in the oven for 30 minutes.

5. Flip the chicken so skin side is up and put back in the oven for 1 hour.

?

What are Subtler Spices Used in Mexican Dishes?

Mexican cooking abounds with subtle spices. Cinnamon, nutmeg, and cloves, for example, are common ingredients in many recipes that don't contain an abundance of hot chili peppers.

This simple dish is wonderful served over white rice with a side of Zucchini with Jalapeños (see page 186).

Fruit-Stewed Turkey

What You Need

6 pitted prunes

1 small yellow onion

¼ cup dried apricots

1 tablespoon olive oil

4 cups cubed cooked turkey (leftovers are great)

1 cup canned or fresh pineapple chunks

½ cup fresh raspberries

1 teaspoon salt

1 teaspoon ground white pepper

What You Do

1. Cut prunes in half. Remove skin from onion and cut into quarters. Cut apricots in half.

2. Put olive oil in a large frying pan and preheat to medium temperature. Add turkey chunks and fry until lightly browned on all sides.

3. Drain oil and add pineapple, apricots, raspberries, prunes, onions, salt, and pepper to the pan. Turn heat to low and cook for 1 hour, stirring periodically.

Nutty Chicken

What You Need

1 cut up chicken (2½–3½ pounds)

½ cup olive oil

¼ cup pepitas

¼ cup sesame seeds

¼ cup pecans

¼ cup slivered almonds

¼ cup pistachio meats

¼ cup filberts

What You Do

1. Preheat oven to 350°F. Brush each piece of chicken with olive oil.

2. Combine all the nuts. In a food processor or nut grinder, grind the nuts into small pieces. Place the nut mixture in a soup bowl and roll each piece of chicken in the nuts. Reserve the remaining nuts.

3. Put the remaining olive oil in a baking pan. Place the chicken, skin side down, in the pan. Bake for 30 minutes. Flip the chicken and sprinkle with remaining nuts. Bake an additional hour.

Authentic Mexican tacos often are served with just meat and salsa.

However, you can add the American fixings such as cheese and lettuce if you'd like.

Chicken Tacos

What You Need

2 cups Spicy Chicken (see page 125)

12 corn tortillas (see Basic Corn Tortillas, page 285), or flour tortillas (see Flour Tortillas, page 286)

What You Do

1. Warm chicken, if necessary.

2. Warm tortillas in ungreased skillet or placa.

3. Fill each tortilla with chicken. Add your favorite salsa.

Is Fruit a Common Ingredient in Mexican Cooking?

Being a warm-weather culture, Mexican dishes frequently use a great deal of fresh fruits. Although those in the United States tend to think of tropical fruits as distinctly Mexican, it's only because most of us don't get them that often. Berries and citrus fruits are common in Mexican diets, too.

Soused Chicken

Serve with white rice.

Ladle the fruit onto the top of the chicken and the rice before serving.

What You Need

½ cup prunes

½ cup dried pears

1 large green apple

1 medium red onion

4 garlic cloves

½ cup black olives

2–3 pounds skinless, boneless chicken breasts

3 cups dry white wine

½ cup raisins

1 teaspoon salt

1 teaspoon black pepper

1 tablespoon dried cilantro

1 cup whole roasted almonds

What You Do

1. Preheat oven to 300°F.

2. Remove pits from prunes and cut in quarters. Cut pears into quarters. Remove stem and core from apple. Cut into 1" pieces. Remove skin from onion and cut into ¼" rounds. Remove skin from garlic cloves and cut into quarters. Cut black olives into quarters.

3. Put chicken in an oven-safe pot. Pour the wine over the top. Add the raisins, prunes, pears, apple, salt, black pepper, red onion, garlic, cilantro, and black olives to the pot.

4. Cover and put in the oven for 2 hours. Remove and add the almonds. Leave uncovered and place back in the oven for 30 minutes.

❓ Is It Soused or Potted?

Mexican dishes that have meat soaking in a sauce, especially an alcohol-based sauce, are often called soused or potted dishes. Funny that those two words have come to mean someone who is drunk, too!

Five-Pepper Chicken Stew

If your local market doesn't have the varieties of chilies mentioned here, experiment with your own variations.

What You Need

4 skinless, boneless chicken breasts

4 fresh jalapeño peppers

4 fresh mulato chilies

4 fresh ancho chilies

1 fresh poblano chili

4 fresh habanero peppers

4 medium tomatoes

4 medium baking potatoes

2 large carrots

½ cup pepitas

¾ cup chopped onion

1 teaspoon garlic paste

What You Do

1. Cut chicken meat into 1" pieces.

2. Remove stems and seeds from chilies and chop chilies into ¼" pieces. Cut tomatoes into quarters. Peel potatoes and cut into 1" pieces. Peel carrot and cut into 1" pieces.

3. Combine all ingredients in a large pot and cook covered on medium-low heat for 3 hours. Stir occasionally.

?

What's a Poblano Chili?

Poblano chilies are one of the largest and mildest-tasting green peppers in the chili category. They are meaty and relatively juicy, which makes them excellent for roasting and baking. Because they are fairly large, they also work well for stuffing.

Marinated Chicken

Serve cold, garnished with pickled vegetables.

What You Need

2 celery stalks

1½ cups vegetable oil

2 cut-up chickens (about 2½ pounds each)

1 cup canned or frozen sliced carrots, thawed or drained

¼ teaspoon garlic paste

⅛ teaspoon thyme

⅛ teaspoon marjoram

1 bay leaf

12 peppercorns

1 teaspoon salt

3 cups vinegar

What You Do

1. Chop celery into 1" pieces.

2. Heat oil to medium in a large skillet. Brown chicken pieces then place them in a large pot. Top with carrots, celery, garlic, thyme, marjoram, bay leaf, peppercorns, and salt. Pour vinegar over all.

3. Remove from heat and let cool to room temperature. Cover and refrigerate for 3–4 hours.

Can I Substitute Turkey for Chicken?

For a lean alternative in your next chicken recipe, substitute turkey. It has much less fat and much more protein than chicken while often being a better per-pound buy at the grocery store.

Garnish with sour cream, guacamole, and chopped green onions.

Enchiladas Rancheros

What You Need

2 garlic cloves

2 medium yellow onions

2 fresh jalapeño peppers

4 large red tomatoes

2 tablespoons vegetable oil

1 teaspoon oregano

¾ pound mushrooms

4 cups cubed cooked chicken

1 pound shredded Monterey jack cheese

1 cup sliced black olives

4 cups sour cream

30 flour tortillas (see Flour Tortillas, page 286)

What You Do

1. Preheat oven to 350°F.

2. Peel garlic and onions and chop finely. Remove stems and seeds from jalapeño peppers and cut into ¼" pieces. Cut tomatoes into ½" pieces.

3. Heat vegetable oil to medium temperature in a medium frying pan. Add garlic, onion, and jalapeño peppers. Cook until onion is transparent. Add tomatoes and oregano. Cook about 5 minutes, stirring frequently.

4. Wash mushrooms and slice thinly. Mix together the chicken, cheese, mushrooms, and black olives. Stir in sour cream.

5. Put 3–4 tablespoons of filling into each tortilla. Roll up and place into a 9" × 13" baking dish. Pour sauce over the top. Bake for 30 minutes or until heated through.

What Mushrooms Can I Substitute?

Different mushrooms have very different tastes. Don't hesitate to substitute soaked exotic dried mushrooms such as wood ear, enoci, and porcini even if the recipe calls for fresh mushrooms.

LEVEL **E**

SERVINGS **8**

Serve with Grilled
Corn on the Cob
(see page 192), and
Fruit Compote (see
page 241).

Cozumel Chicken

What You Need

1 tablespoon butter

8 large skinless boneless chicken breasts

8 Key limes

2 lemons

1 cup orange juice

1 cup Red Chili Sauce (see page 17)

What You Do

1. Preheat oven to 325°F.

2. Melt butter on medium heat in a large skillet. Add boneless chicken breasts and cook until brown on one side. Flip and brown on the other.

3. Wash limes and lemons but do not peel. Slice as thinly as possible.

4. Put chicken in an ovenproof baking dish. Top with lime and lemon slices. Pour orange juice over the top.

5. Cover with aluminum foil and bake about 1 hour or until chicken is tender.

6. Remove lime and lemon slices and pour Red Chili Sauce over chicken. Heat for 5 more minutes.

When served with fresh fruit, this makes a perfect lunch for a large group.

Egg-Stuffed Rolls v

What You Need

1 medium yellow onion

2 pounds shredded Cheddar cheese

1 can sliced black olives

6 hardboiled eggs

½ cup sliced canned jalapeño peppers

1 cup red tomato salsa (see Tomato Salsa, page 12)

1 cup vegetable oil

¼ cup vinegar

1 tablespoon garlic salt

3 dozen small French rolls

What You Do

1. Peel onion and cut into ¼" pieces.

2. Combine cheese, olives, onions, eggs, jalapeño peppers, tomato salsa, vegetable oil, vinegar, and garlic salt in a medium mixing bowl. Cover and refrigerate 8–12 hours.

3. Preheat oven to 300°F.

4. Cut off tops of French rolls and dig out some of the bread. Fill with mixture and wrap stuffed rolls with waxed paper.

5. Place on a cookie sheet and bake for 1 hour.

How Do I Keep Grated Cheese from Sticking?

To save money, buy blocks of cheese and grate them yourself. To keep the cheese from sticking together, add a little cornstarch and toss cheese until mixed through.

Serve with a side
of fresh fruit to
make this a
complete meal.

Eggs in Potato Shells   v

What You Need

1 large baking potato
(at least 8 ounces)

2 tablespoons sour cream

1 small yellow onion

1 teaspoon butter

2 tablespoons chopped
fresh green bell pepper

1 tablespoon drained
canned jalapeño pepper

1 medium red tomato

2 eggs

1 cup shredded Cheddar
cheese

What You Do

1. Preheat oven to 350°F.

2. Cut potato in half lengthwise. Using a spoon, scoop
   out inside of potato, leaving ¼" thick shell. In a small
   mixing bowl, combine potato pulp and 1 tablespoon
   sour cream. Mash and set aside.

3. Peel onion and cut onion and tomato into ¼" pieces.
   In a small frying pan, melt butter. Add onion,
   green bell pepper, and jalapeño pepper. Cook over
   medium-high heat, stirring frequently, until vegetables are tender. Add tomatoes and continue cooking, stirring frequently. Cook about 3 minutes.

4. Add about half of the cooked vegetables to potato
   pulp mixture and stir to thoroughly combine. Spoon
   half of mixture into each reserved potato shell.

5. Place potato halves in a 1-quart casserole. Using the
   back of a spoon, make an indentation in the center
   of each potato. Break one egg into a dish, then slide
   it into the indentation. Repeat with second potato.

6. Bake for 50 minutes. Top with Cheddar cheese
   and return to oven for 5 minutes or until cheese
   is melted. Top each egg with remaining vegetable
   mixture and sour cream right before serving.

LEVEL **M**

SERVINGS **6**

Serve as a side dish for Mexican Meat Loaf (see page 108).

Chili Egg Noodles ᵥ

What You Need

1 (10-ounce) package fresh egg noodles

½ teaspoon chili powder

2 dried ancho chilies

1 cup whipping cream

1 cup shredded Cheddar cheese

½ teaspoon paprika

What You Do

1. Bring 2 quarts of water to a boil in a large saucepan. Add noodles and chili powder. Boil for 10 minutes. Drain and rinse in cold water. Preheat oven to 350°F.

2. Break off stems and shake out seeds from chilies. Cut into quarters and put in a blender or food processor. Add whipping cream. Blend until chilies are finely chopped.

3. Layer in a greased 2-quart casserole: noodles, cheese, then sauce. Sprinkle top with paprika.

4. Bake 30 minutes or until bubbling hot.

Chicken in Nutty Green Sauce

Have fun with this dish by experimenting with different types and amounts of chili peppers.

What You Need

1 cut-up chicken	½ cup blanched almond slivers
2 cups chicken stock (see Chicken Stock, page 124)	½ cup chopped walnuts
6 habanero chilies	1 teaspoon garlic paste
1 medium yellow onion	1 teaspoon salt
6 green tomatoes	1 teaspoon black pepper
1 green bell pepper	1 tablespoon olive oil
1 bunch fresh cilantro	½ cup cooking sherry

What You Do

1. Preheat oven to 300°F.

2. Place chicken and chicken stock in an ovenproof covered casserole. Cook for 30 minutes.

3. Remove stems and seeds from chilies. Remove skin from onion and cut into quarters. Remove stems from tomatoes and cut into quarters. Remove stems and seeds from green bell pepper and cut into quarters. Remove and discard stems from cilantro.

4. Combine the chilies, almonds, walnuts, onion, garlic paste, tomatoes, bell pepper, cilantro, salt, black pepper, olive oil, and cooking sherry in a mixing bowl. Scoop out about 1 cup at a time and place in the blender or food processor. Blend until all ingredients are melded but not puréed. Repeat until all the ingredients are blended.

5. Drain the chicken stock from the chicken. Pour the sauce over the chicken, cover, and replace in the oven. Cook for 1½ hours.

LEVEL **M**

SERVINGS **8**

Cocoa Turkey

Try this for a unique Thanksgiving treat. You'll be surprised how good chocolate and turkey meat go together!

What You Need

1 medium turkey (8–10 pounds)

1 medium red onion

4 garlic cloves

¾ cup vegetable oil

2 cups powdered cocoa

1 teaspoon cinnamon

¼ teaspoon anise

What You Do

1. Preheat oven to 350°F.

2. Thaw the turkey, remove the giblets from the cavity, and wash the cavity thoroughly.

3. Remove the skin from the onion and chop into ¼" pieces. Remove the skin from the garlic and chop. Stir the onion and garlic into ¼ cup vegetable oil and, using a paper towel, rub the inside of the turkey cavity with the garlic and onion mixture. Leave all the garlic and onion pieces inside the cavity.

4. Mix the powdered cocoa, cinnamon, and anise into ½ cup vegetable oil. Use this to baste the turkey.

5. Place the turkey in the oven and baste every 15 minutes for 3 hours. Remove the turkey and let it sit for 30 minutes before serving.

Can I Use Cocoa as a Spice?

While Americans think of cocoa only in terms of chocolate, many Mexican dishes use it as a main spice. They will mix it with cheeses, meats, and even vegetables. Although it can take some getting used to, it's definitely worth trying.

Serve with
Pineapple Coconut
Salad
(see page 94).

Chicken Achiote

What You Need

1 cut-up chicken (2½–2⅓ pounds)

4 garlic cloves

1 medium red onion

4 jalapeño peppers

2 tablespoons achiote paste

½ cup white grapefruit juice

½ cup red cooking sherry

1 cup green seedless grapes

What You Do

1. Remove skin from chicken pieces, but not bones.

2. Remove skin from garlic. Remove skin from onion and cut into quarters. Remove stems (but not seeds) from jalapeño peppers. Put achiote paste, grapefruit juice, garlic, onion, chili peppers and cooking sherry in blender or food processor. Blend on medium setting until all ingredients are melded.

3. Place chicken in a mixing bowl. Cover with sauce. Cover bowl and place in refrigerator for 6–12 hours.

4. Preheat oven to 350°F.

5. Cut grapes in half. Remove chicken and place in a baking dish. Cover with grapes. Cook uncovered for 1 hour.

What's Achiote?

Achiote is a blend of ground annatto seeds, garlic, black pepper, other spices, and vinegar. It is common in Yucatan cooking but has migrated into middle Mexican cooking as well. It leaves food (as well as clothing, plastic cookware, and anything else it touches) a bright orange color.

Chicken Tablecloth Stainer

LEVEL **M**

SERVINGS **8**

Mexicans love to have whimsical names for their meals. This one obviously got its name from the wonderful red color the chili powder gives it.

Serve with Turnip & Mustard Leaf Rolls (see page 203).

What You Need

½ cup canned pineapple chunks

1 medium red apple

1 large, firm banana

1 medium white onion

1 garlic clove

½ pound link sausages

2 cut-up chickens (about 2½ pounds each)

1 tablespoon chili powder

2 cups canned tomatoes

½ cup whole blanched almonds

¼ teaspoon cinnamon

⅛ teaspoon ground cloves

2 cups chicken stock (see Chicken Stock, page 124)

2 teaspoons salt

1 teaspoon ground black pepper

What You Do

1. Drain juice from pineapple. Peel apple, core, and slice into ¼"-thick crescents. Peel banana and cut into ¼"-thick rounds. Peel onion and slice in half. Peel garlic.

2. Fry sausage until brown in a medium frying pan (reserve grease). Put chicken and sausages in a large, heavy kettle. Add pineapple, apple, and banana to the top.

3. Combine chili powder, onion, garlic, tomatoes with their juice, almonds, cinnamon, and cloves in a blender or food processor. Blend to a purée.

4. Heat the grease in the skillet in which the sausages were cooked. Add the blended sauce and cook about 5 minutes, stirring constantly. Stir in chicken stock. Add salt and pepper.

5. Pour sauce over chicken. Cover and simmer over low heat 1 hour or until chicken is tender.

Duck in Prune Sauce

LEVEL **M**

SERVINGS **6**

Serve with Green Beans with Pine Nuts (see page 188).

If you can't find a duckling already cut into serving pieces, ask to have it cut at the market.

What You Need

2 cups pitted prunes

¼ cup raisins

1 cup dry sherry

1 large white onion

2 garlic cloves

4 tomatillos

1 cut-up duckling (4–5 pounds)

1 cup flour

½ cup butter

1 teaspoon salt

½ teaspoon black pepper

½ teaspoon nutmeg

What You Do

1. Preheat oven to 325°F. Cut the prunes into ¼" pieces. Put the prunes and raisins in a small bowl and add the sherry. Let soak at least 2 hours. Peel onion and chop into ¼" pieces. Peel the garlic cloves and mince. Peel tomatillos and chop into ¼" pieces. Roll duck pieces in flour.

2. Heat the butter in a large frying pan over medium heat. Add duck pieces and cook until browned on both sides. Sprinkle with salt and pepper during the last couple minutes of browning. Place duck pieces in a large ovenproof casserole. Do not drain grease from frying pan.

3. Put the onions in the frying pan and cook on medium heat until they are limp but not brown. Stir in the garlic, tomatillos, and nutmeg. Pour over the duck. Cover casserole and cook 1½ hours. Uncover casserole and cook an additional 15 minutes.

How are Nuts Used in Mexican Cooking?

Being in a subtropical climate means Mexicans have a much greater access to a large variety of nuts. As a result, they often use them as the equivalent of flour, as a thickening agent for sauces, or as a batter.

Serve with white rice and Carrot Chili Pepper Salad (see page 91).

Green Chicken with Almond Sauce

What You Need

4 canned tomatillos

4 fresh serrano chilies

1 large white onion

1 handful fresh coriander

1 handful fresh parsley

1 cup blanched almonds

1 cup flour

1 teaspoon garlic salt

1 teaspoon white pepper

1 cut-up chicken

2 tablespoons olive oil

1 cup chicken stock (see Chicken Stock, page 124)

1 cup white cooking sherry

What You Do

1. Preheat oven to 350°F. Quarter tomatillos. Remove stems from chilies and quarter. Peel onion and quarter. Cut thick stems off coriander and parsley. Chop almonds into small pieces.

2. Combine flour, salt, and white pepper. Moisten chicken with water and roll in the flour mixture.

3. Heat olive oil to medium temperature in a frying pan. Add chicken. Fry until chicken is golden brown on all sides. Place chicken in an ovenproof casserole.

4. Put chicken stock, tomatillos, serrano chilies, cooking sherry, onion, coriander, and parsley in a blender. Blend on medium speed until puréed. Stir in almonds. Pour mixture over chicken. Bake for 1 hour.

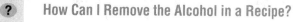

How Can I Remove the Alcohol in a Recipe?

If you don't want alcohol in your noncooked recipe, take slightly more than you need for the recipe and cook it over medium heat for a few minutes. The alcohol will evaporate but you will be left with all the flavor.

Creamy Chicken with Mushrooms

LEVEL **M**

SERVINGS **4**

Serve with
Cucumber Mousse
(see page 82), for
an interesting blend
of flavors.

What You Need

1 pound fresh mushrooms

1 large red onion

1 garlic clove

2 medium red tomatoes

1 red bell pepper

2 fresh jalapeño peppers

4 boneless, skinless chicken breasts

2 cups chicken stock (see Chicken Stock, page 124)

1 sprig epazote

½ cup heavy cream

What You Do

1. Preheat oven to 350°F. Clean mushrooms and slice thinly. Peel onion and slice into ¼" rounds. Peel garlic and quarter. Peel tomatoes and remove stems. Cut into quarters. Remove stem and seeds from red bell pepper and quarter. Remove stems and seeds from jalapeño peppers and cut into ¼" rounds.

2. Place chicken breasts in an ovenproof casserole. Add mushrooms and onion slices on top. Cover with 1 cup chicken stock. Cover casserole and bake for 1 hour.

3. In the meantime, combine 1 cup chicken stock, garlic, tomatoes, red bell pepper, jalapeño peppers, and epazote in a blender. Blend on medium speed until puréed. Pour mixture into a medium skillet at medium heat. Gently stir in heavy cream until it is well mixed, making sure mixture does not boil.

4. Pour creamy mixture over chicken. Replace cover and bake an additional 15 minutes.

LEVEL **M**
SERVINGS **4**

Serve with sour cream, Guacamole (see page 16), and Tomato Salsa (see page 12).

Chimichangas

What You Need

1 pound lean ground beef

½ cup chopped onion

½ teaspoon ground black pepper

1 teaspoon garlic salt

½ cup canned chopped jalapeño peppers, drained

1 teaspoon chili powder

¼ teaspoon cayenne pepper

½ teaspoon oregano

½ pound shredded Colby cheese

8 flour tortillas (see Flour Tortillas, page 286)

2 cups vegetable oil

1 medium red tomato

What You Do

1. Place ground beef and onions in a medium-sized frying pan. Fry on medium heat until meat is brown and onions are translucent. Drain grease.

2. Add jalapeño peppers, chili powder, black pepper, garlic salt, cayenne pepper, and oregano. Simmer for 10 minutes.

3. Put 2 to 3 tablespoons of mixture in the middle of each tortilla. Add 1 tablespoon of grated cheese on top. Fold tortillas and secure with toothpicks.

4. Heat 2 cups vegetable oil to medium-high in a large skillet. Add 2 or 3 tortillas at a time. Fry quickly until golden brown on each side.

Southwestern Fried Chicken

LEVEL **M**

SERVINGS **4**

Serve with Calabacitas (see page 196), for a well-balanced, slightly spicy meal.

What You Need

3 pieces white bread

1 bunch fresh cilantro

2 garlic cloves

2 eggs

2 tablespoons cornmeal

2 tablespoons pine nuts

1½ teaspoons ground oregano

½ teaspoon salt

¼ teaspoon cayenne pepper

¼ teaspoon ground cumin

⅛ teaspoon ground cloves

2 tablespoons prepared yellow mustard

1 tablespoon water

2 teaspoons honey

4 chicken breasts

¼ teaspoon ground black pepper

2 tablespoons butter

What You Do

1. Preheat oven to 400°F.

2. Tear bread into 1" pieces. Remove stems from cilantro. Peel garlic. Separate eggs and discard yolks.

3. Blend bread, cilantro, cornmeal, pine nuts, garlic, cumin, oregano, ¼ teaspoon salt, cayenne pepper, and ground cloves in a food processor or blender until you have fine crumbs. Add egg whites and mix until crumbs are moist. Spread crumb mixture on a plate.

4. Mix together mustard, water, and honey in a small bowl. Brush over chicken with a pastry brush. Sprinkle chicken with pepper and ¼ teaspoon salt. Dip chicken one piece at a time in bread mixture, pressing lightly so mixture sticks.

5. Melt butter in a 9" × 11" baking dish. Place chicken breasts skin-side down in butter. Bake 20 minutes. Flip chicken and bake an additional 20 minutes.

Yucatan Tamale Pie

For a stronger flavor, remove the vegetables from the stock pot and drain the liquid. Mix the vegetables with the chicken pieces while placing them in the casserole.

What You Need

½ cup lard

3 cups cornmeal

4 jalapeño peppers

4 medium ripe tomatoes

1 (3–4 pound) chicken

½ cup chopped onion

½ teaspoon garlic paste

1 teaspoon oregano

¼ teaspoon dried cilantro

½ teaspoon brown sugar

4 cups chicken broth (see Chicken Stock, page 124)

What You Do

1. Preheat oven to 350°F.

2. Combine lard and cornmeal, adding small amounts of water until the dough is soft enough to work with. Grease an ovenproof casserole and line the bottom and sides with the dough.

3. Remove stem and seeds from jalapeño peppers and chop into ¼" pieces. Cut tomatoes into 1" pieces.

4. Place chicken, onions, garlic paste, tomatoes, jalapeño peppers, oregano, cilantro, and brown sugar into a large stock pot. Pour chicken broth over everything.

5. Bring to a boil. Reduce heat to medium and simmer covered for 1 hour.

6. Remove chicken and cool. Reserve the broth. Remove the bones and skin from the chicken and tear the meat into strips about 1" wide. Layer the chicken on the dough in the casserole.

7. Bake covered for 1 hour. Pour 1 cup of chicken broth over the pie before serving.

Chicken with Mushrooms

Serve with Pineapple Coconut Salad (see page 94), and Refried Beans (see page 211).

What You Need

1 pound fresh mushrooms

1 garlic clove

1 medium yellow onion

¼ cup olive oil

2 cut-up chickens

2 cups canned diced tomatoes with juice

2 canned green chilies

1 cup chicken stock (see Chicken Stock, page 124)

1½ teaspoon salt

1 cup sour cream

What You Do

1. Wash mushrooms and slice thinly. Peel garlic and onion and cut onion into quarters.

2. Heat oil to medium in a frying pan. Fry chicken until golden brown. Put chicken in a saucepot. Cook mushrooms in the oil remaining in the frying pan. Spoon mushrooms over chicken. Do not drain oil.

3. Combine tomatoes with their juice, chilies, onion, and garlic in an electric blender or food processor. Blend until puréed. Pour purée into the skillet with the oil. Bring to a boil and cook about 5 minutes. Stir in chicken stock and salt.

4. Pour sauce over chicken and mushrooms. Cover and cook over low heat until chicken is tender, about 1 hour. Just before serving, stir in sour cream and heat through, but do not boil.

Do I Have to Peel the Potatoes?

Potato skins contain many vitamins not found in the "meat" of the potato. Unless your recipe calls for a clean, "white" look, leave the skins on and savor the extra nutrition.

Serve this as a dessert at your next traditional Mexican meal.

Royal Eggs v

What You Need

¼ cup raisins

½ cup dry sherry

12 eggs

2 cups sugar

1 cup water

1 cinnamon stick

¼ cup slivered almonds

What You Do

1. Preheat oven to 325°F.

2. Soak raisins in ¼ cup of the sherry. Separate eggs and discard whites.

3. Beat egg yolks until they form a ribbon when poured from the beater. Pour into a buttered shallow pan. Set this pan in another larger pan with about 1" of water in it.

4. Bake for 20 to 25 minutes, or until set. Remove from oven and cool on a wire rack. When cool, cut into 1" cubes.

5. While the eggs are cooling, combine sugar, water, and cinnamon stick in a saucepan and bring to boil. Reduce heat to medium-low and simmer about 5 minutes, stirring until all sugar is dissolved. Remove cinnamon stick.

6. Carefully place egg cubes in sauce. Continue simmering over very low heat until cubes are well-saturated with the syrup. Add soaked raisins and remaining sherry. Sprinkle with slivered almonds.

?

Where Do Some Mexican Recipes Originate From?

Many of the Mexican recipes that combine European ingredients such as sherry with traditional Mexican ingredients such as eggs actually were invented by Spanish nuns who first came to Mexico as missionaries.

This is wonderful served with Refried Beans (see page 211), or Red Rice (see page 212).

These are also great cooked on the grill.

Key Lime Chicken

What You Need

6 Key limes

1 chipotle pepper

¼ cup lemon juice

¼ cup orange juice

2 tablespoons vegetable oil

1 teaspoon salt

1 cup Green Tomato Salsa (see page 13)

4 skin-on chicken breasts

What You Do

1. Remove the rind from 4 of the Key limes and discard. Remove the stem and seeds from the chipotle pepper and discard. Combine the lemon juice, orange juice, chili, oil, salt, Green Tomato Salsa, and 4 of the Key limes in a blender or food processor. Blend on medium until you have a nice purée—it should be thick with no obvious chunks. Transfer the blend to a pot and cook on medium heat about 15 minutes. Let cool.

3. Debone the chicken breasts and place in a large mixing bowl. Pour the sauce over the top. Cover and refrigerate for 6–12 hours.

4. Preheat broiler. Place on the grill or broiler and use the marinade to baste the chicken every few minutes. Turn the chicken over when the first side gets brown and cook again. Chicken breasts take from 10–20 minutes to cook thoroughly. Cut into one to make sure the breast is cooked through before serving.

5. Cut remaining 2 Key limes in half. Before serving, squeeze the juice from one half onto each breast.

? What's a Chipotle Pepper?

Chipotle peppers are dried, smoked red jalapeño peppers. Although spicy, the flavor that lingers is the smoky taste. As a result, they will flavor something more than any other chili pepper.

Squabs in Orange Sauce

Use the juice in the bottom of the pan as a dipping sauce for the meat.

What You Need

1 medium white onion

1 garlic clove

2 tablespoons pecans

2 medium red tomatoes

4 squabs

½ cup butter

1 cup freshly squeezed orange juice

½ cup dry white wine

½ teaspoon thyme

1 tablespoon grated orange rind

What You Do

1. Preheat oven to 325°F. Peel onion and cut into ¼" rounds. Peel garlic, and chop garlic and pecans finely. Remove stems from tomatoes and chop into ¼" pieces.

2. Split each squab in half lengthwise, leaving it in one piece. Melt butter in a large frying pan on medium heat. Cook each squab until golden brown on all sides. Do not drain grease. Place squabs in an oven-proof casserole dish. It's fine if they overlap.

3. Put the onion and garlic in the frying pan and cook until the onion is limp but not brown. Reduce heat to low. Add orange juice, tomatoes, wine, pecans, and thyme. Cook for 5 minutes, stirring occasionally. Pour over squabs.

4. Cover casserole and bake for 1½ hours.

5. Arrange squabs on a serving platter. Sprinkle with orange rind.

Stuffed Turkey

Make a gravy by adding flour to pan drippings then stirring in equal amounts broth and red wine. Cook until bubbly and the desired thickness. Season with salt and pepper.

To stuff the turkey, spoon stuffing into cavities and secure with skewers or twine. Put turkey breast-side up on a rack in a shallow roasting pan. Cover with a double thickness of cheesecloth soaked in butter.

What You Need

1 turkey (12–16 pounds)	3 medium carrots
1 teaspoon salt	3 bananas
1 teaspoon black pepper	3 medium red apples
1 tablespoon lemon juice	5 slices bacon
1 cup butter	3 pounds ground pork
1 medium yellow onion	½ cup tomato paste
1 garlic clove	¾ cup raisins
¾ cup blanched almonds	2 teaspoons sugar
½ cup black olives	1 teaspoon cinnamon
6 fresh jalapeño peppers	

What You Do

1. Clean turkey. Sprinkle inside and out with salt and pepper then drizzle with lemon juice. Preheat oven to 325°F. Melt butter in a small pan on low heat then soak about 1 yard of cheesecloth in melted butter.

2. Peel onion and chop. Peel garlic clove and mince. Chop almonds. Chop black olives. Remove stems and seeds from jalapeño peppers and chop. Peel carrots and slice. Peel bananas and slice. Peel apples, remove cores, and chop.

3. Fry bacon until brown at medium heat in a frying pan. Remove bacon and place on paper towels to cool. Brown onion and garlic in the fat in the skillet. Add ground pork and fry until browned. Drain excess fat.

4. Add tomato paste, almonds, olives, jalapeño peppers, carrots, bananas, apples, raisins, sugar, and cinnamon. Cook several minutes on medium heat, stirring frequently. Mix in bacon. Let cool and stuff turkey. Roast turkey for 4–5 hours or until meat thermometer reaches 180°F in thickest part of the breast.

Chapter 7
Fish and Seafood

Sea Bass with Filberts

This is excellent served with Zucchini with Jalapeños (see page 186).

What You Need

6 large sea bass fillets (6–10 ounces each)

1 tablespoon lemon juice

1 medium white onion

¼ cup olive oil

12 chopped green olives

¼ cup canned, chopped pimientos

½ teaspoon salt

1 teaspoon ground black pepper

½ teaspoon crushed coriander

2 tablespoons orange juice

½ cup crushed filberts

¼ cup chopped parsley

What You Do

1. Preheat oven to 375°F.

2. Lay fillets in an ovenproof baking pan. Sprinkle with lemon juice.

3. Remove skin from onion and chop into ¼" pieces.

4. Cook onion in olive oil on medium heat in a small skillet for 3 minutes. Add the olives, pimientos, salt, black pepper, and coriander and cook for an additional 3 minutes.

5. Remove the mixture from heat. Add the orange juice and filberts. Stir well.

6. Pour mixture over fish and place in oven for 30 minutes or until fish flakes easily. Sprinkle with parsley before serving.

Shark Steak with Tomato Sauce

Serve with Red Rice
(see page 212), and
fresh fruit.

What You Need

4 medium shark steaks (about 6 ounces each)

½ teaspoon salt

½ teaspoon ground black pepper

1 teaspoon olive oil

4 garlic cloves

4 scallions

2 habanero peppers

2 tablespoons chopped fresh cilantro

1 cup Green Tomato Salsa (see page 13)

What You Do

1. Preheat oven to 350°F.

2. Sprinkle both sides of shark steaks with salt and pepper. Grease the bottom of a 9" × 13" baking pan with olive oil. Place steaks in pan.

3. Remove skin from garlic cloves and scallions. Slice thinly. Remove stem and seeds from peppers and slice thinly. Top steaks with garlic, scallions, and pepper pieces. Sprinkle cilantro on top.

4. Pour Green Tomato Salsa over steaks evenly. Place in oven and cook for 20 minutes.

Serve with a fresh
fruit salad for a light
summer meal.

Grilled Swordfish

What You Need

1 teaspoon chili powder

2 tablespoons lime juice

1 teaspoon dried oregano

1 tablespoon chopped fresh cilantro

¼ cup canned anchovies

½ teaspoon ground cayenne pepper

1 teaspoon salt

1 cup Basic Picante Sauce (see page 15)

4 large swordfish fillets (about 6 ounces each)

What You Do

1. Preheat grill to medium-high heat.
2. Add chili powder, lime juice, dried oregano, fresh cilantro, anchovies, cayenne pepper, and salt to picante sauce.
3. Place fillets on grill and baste liberally with the sauce, reserving about ¼ cup for serving. Turn once and baste again.
4. When fillets are done, drizzle remaining sauce over the top.

Smothered Shrimp

This is excellent
served with a variety
of cheeses
and wines.

What You Need

1 small white onion

½ cup olive oil

1 teaspoon garlic paste

½ cup canned chopped jalapeño peppers

1 cup canned diced tomatoes, drained

1 cup canned chopped tomatillos

¼ cup dry cooking sherry

2 pounds frozen cooked shrimp, thawed

What You Do

1. Remove skin from onion and chop finely. Chop tomatoes into ¼" pieces.

2. Heat the olive oil in a medium frying pan. Add the garlic, onion, and jalapeños. Cook on medium heat until the onions are limp but not brown. Add the tomatoes and tomatillos, including the juice from the tomatillos. Continue cooking at medium heat, stirring constantly, for 15 minutes. Stir in the cooking sherry.

3. Preheat oven to 300°F. Arrange shrimp in a large baking pan. Pour the sauce over the shrimp. Place the pan in the oven for 15 minutes.

What Fish Tastes Best?

Because most Mexican fish recipes call for adding sauces and spices to the fish, look for a firm, mild-flavored, white-fleshed fish that holds up well to cooking. Bass, flounder, shark, swordfish, and red snapper all work well. Some fish can have surprisingly strong flavors so if you want to try a new fish, take a small piece home and steam it to see if you like the flavor before putting it in your recipe.

Crab with Spinach & Rice

Serve with fresh Flour Tortillas (see page 286), and assorted fresh fruits.

What You Need

1 small yellow onion

2 pounds crab meat

6 cups rice, cooked in chicken broth (see Chicken Stock, page 124)

2 cups frozen or canned spinach, thawed or drained

½ teaspoon garlic paste

1 teaspoon chopped canned jalapeño pepper

1 teaspoon salt

1 teaspoon ground black pepper

1 cup shredded mozzarella cheese

What You Do

1. Remove skin from onion and cut into ¼" pieces.

2. Preheat oven to 350°F.

3. In a large mixing bowl, combine crab meat, rice, spinach, onion, garlic paste, jalapeño pepper, salt, and black pepper until well mixed.

4. Spread mixture in a large baking dish. Top with grated mozzarella cheese. Bake for 1 hour.

Can I Substitute "Imitation Crab" for the Real Thing?

Many people try to substitute "imitation crab" for the real thing. These inexpensive "sea legs" are actually a fine substitute if you are eating the meat right away. However, they quickly lose their flavor and soon taste like gummy noodles. You're better off paying for the real thing.

Halibut Ceviche

What You Need

1½ to 2 pounds fresh halibut

½ cup lime juice

1 small red onion

2 serrano chilies

1 large red tomato

½ cup fresh cilantro leaves

¼ cup sliced green olives stuffed with pimientos

½ cup orange juice

1 teaspoon salt

What You Do

1. Cut the halibut into ½" cubes. Combine the fish and lime juice in a small glass or ceramic container. Cover and refrigerate for 1 hour.

2. Remove skin from onion and cut into ¼" pieces. Remove stem and seeds from serrano chilies and cut into ¼" pieces. Chop tomato into ¼" pieces. Reserve juice. Chop cilantro into ¼" pieces.

3. Drain lime juice and put fish in a medium-sized mixing bowl. Add the onions, chilies, olives, tomatoes with their juice, orange juice, and salt. Stir well. Refrigerate in a glass or ceramic container for 4–12 hours.

Do I Have to Eat the Fish Raw with Ceviche?

Ceviche is always served with raw fish because the lime juice effectively cooks the outside layer of flesh. However, if you're squeamish about eating raw fish, steam the fish chunks for five minutes to make sure they are fully cooked. You will lose some of the authentic flavor of a true ceviche but it will still taste marvelous.

Shrimp in Vinaigrette

What You Need

1 small red onion

1 jalapeño pepper

1–2 cups red wine vinegar

1 teaspoon sugar

½ teaspoon salt

½ teaspoon ground white pepper

2 pounds frozen cooked shrimp, thawed

½ teaspoon cayenne pepper

What You Do

1. Remove skin from onion and chop onion into ¼" pieces. Remove stem and seeds from jalapeño pepper and chop into ¼" pieces.

2. Mix 1 cup red wine vinegar, chopped onions, jalapeños, sugar, salt, and ground white pepper.

3. Put shrimp in a large glass or ceramic dish and sprinkle with cayenne pepper. Pour sauce over the top, making sure all shrimp are covered. If you need more sauce, add the remaining cup of red wine vinegar.

4. Put in refrigerator and chill for 4–12 hours before serving.

LEVEL **E**

SERVINGS **8**

To add authenticity and deeper, fishier flavor, cook the fish with the head and skin on. After 15 minutes of simmering, remove the head, skin, and bones and return the meat to the pot. Cook another 5 minutes before serving.

Puerto Vallarta's Catfish Soup

What You Need

4 fresh jalapeño peppers

6 medium carrots

½ chopped onion

4 cups canned whole tomatoes

¾ teaspoon garlic paste

1 teaspoon oregano

1 teaspoon salt

½ teaspoon ground black pepper

½ teaspoon paprika

2 pounds catfish fillets

What You Do

1. Remove stem and seeds from jalapeño peppers and chop into ¼" pieces. Peel carrots and cut into ¼" rounds.

2. Fill a large pot with 2 quarts water. Add onion, tomatoes, jalapeño peppers, garlic, carrots, oregano, salt, black pepper, and paprika to the pot. Stir gently. Heat on high until boiling. Reduce heat to medium and simmer uncovered until tomatoes have disintegrated and carrots are tender.

3. Cut catfish fillets into 1" cubes. Add cubes to the broth and simmer for 15 minutes.

Serve with Spinach Salad (see page 89), and baked sweet potatoes.

When the fish is done frying, the flesh should be opaque and flake easily with a fork.

Sea Bass from Veracruz

What You Need

4 large sea bass fillets

½ cup flour

1 teaspoon salt

½ teaspoon white pepper

½ teaspoon black pepper

½ cup olive oil

1 medium yellow onion

2 garlic cloves

3 fresh largo chilies

2 cups canned tomato paste

½ cup sliced black olives

¼ teaspoon cinnamon

¼ teaspoon ground cloves

1 tablespoon lime juice

1 teaspoon sugar

What You Do

1. Coat the sea bass fillets with flour. Sprinkle both sides with salt and white pepper. Heat ¼ cup olive oil in a frying pan. Add fish fillets and fry on each side until thoroughly cooked and golden brown. Remove from heat and set aside.

2. Peel onion and chop into ¼" pieces. Peel garlic and mince. Remove seeds and stem from chilies and chop into ¼" pieces.

3. Add remaining ¼ cup olive oil to the frying pan and heat to medium. Add onion, garlic, and chilies. Cook until onion is limp. Add tomato paste, olives, cinnamon, black pepper, and ground cloves. Cook until heated through. Add lime juice and sugar. Stir gently. Reduce heat to low. Add fish fillets. Cover and cook for 5 minutes.

?

How Do I Cook With Cilantro?

Cilantro is a common weed that is used as a spice in Mexican cooking as well as other warm-climate dishes. It has a rather strong and unusual taste that becomes stronger as it is cooked. If you're not sure about the taste, add just a little bit at the end of the cooking process.

LEVEL **M**

SERVINGS **4**

While this is excellent served with white rice for a light dinner, it also is good served cold atop a bed of mixed greens.

If you must substitute lobster tails for langoustines, cut them into 1" slices.

Soused Langoustines

What You Need

6 capers

½ cup fresh lime juice

½ cup dry white wine

1 ½ teaspoons garlic paste

½ teaspoon cayenne pepper

½ teaspoon salt

2 pounds langoustines

What You Do

1. Chop capers finely.

2. Combine lime juice, white wine, capers, garlic paste, cayenne pepper, and salt.

3. Put langoustines in a medium-sized frying pan. Pour liquid mixture over the top. Slowly bring the mixture to a simmer at medium temperature. Simmer for 5 minutes or until the langoustines are opaque.

4. Remove from the heat. Pour the entire mixture into a bowl and refrigerate for 24 hours.

5. Drain liquid and reheat langoustines before serving.

What Are Langoustines?

Langoustines are small lobsters commonly found in tropical climates. They are excellent for cooking in stews and soups because the pieces of flesh are so small that they easily take up the spices. You likely won't find langoustines in the shell anywhere except the southern coastal states but fresh or freshly frozen usually work just fine in a recipe.

Red Snapper with Pecan Sauce

This unique blend of flavors is suitable for almost any white fish.

It also works for seafood such as shrimp and scallops.

What You Need

1 cup chicken stock (see Chicken Stock, page 124)

1 cup water

4 red snapper fillets (6–10 ounces each)

1 small yellow onion

2 garlic cloves

1 cup pecans

1 teaspoon salt

1 teaspoon saffron powder

2 Key limes

What You Do

1. Add water to chicken stock. Pour into a large frying pan and bring to a boil. Add the fillets. Reduce heat to medium-low and cook until the fish flakes easily with a fork. Lift the fish out and place on a serving platter.

2. Remove skin from onion and garlic cloves. Cut onion into quarters.

3. Put the garlic cloves, onion, ¾ cup of pecans, ½ cup of remaining broth from the frying pan, salt, and saffron powder into a blender or food processor and blend at medium speed for about 2 minutes or until you have a smooth purée.

4. Heat the sauce in a medium saucepan at medium heat. Do not let it boil. Pour the sauce over the fish fillets. Top with the remaining pecans. Squeeze the juice from the 2 limes on top right before serving.

? What is Saffron?

Pure saffron is one of the rarest spices in the world. It has a very subtle yet distinctive flavor that is brought out in fish dishes. Saffron powder usually is diluted with other ingredients that help carry the flavor of the saffron throughout the food.

LEVEL **M**

SERVINGS **4**

Tuna Steaks with Chili Sauce

To add some color to this dish, garnish the fish with fresh sprigs of parsley or cilantro.

What You Need

1 cup water

1 cup chicken stock (see Chicken Stock, page 124)

4 tuna steaks (6–10 ounces each)

1 medium yellow onion

2 garlic cloves

8 chili peppers, your choice (see below)

1 teaspoon salt

½ teaspoon cayenne pepper

1 teaspoon white pepper

4 tablespoons olive oil

What You Do

1. Add 1 cup water to 1 cup chicken stock. Pour into a large frying pan and bring to a boil. Add the tuna steaks. Reduce heat to medium-low and cook until the fish flakes easily with a fork. Lift the fish out and place on a serving platter.

2. Remove skin from onion and garlic cloves. Cut onion into quarters. Remove the seeds and stem from the chili peppers. Cut in quarters.

3. Put the garlic cloves, onion, chili peppers, ½ cup of remaining broth from the frying pan, olive oil, salt, cayenne pepper, and white pepper into a blender or food processor and blend at medium speed for about 2 minutes or until you have a smooth purée.

4. Heat the sauce in a medium saucepan at medium heat. Do not let it boil. Pour the sauce over the fish fillets.

How Do I Choose Chili Peppers?

Chili peppers can be fun to experiment with as there are so many varieties available today. Don't hesitate to try something new. (See Chapter 1 for a guide to their hotness.) You will soon get beyond the heat of the first bite and discover a wide range of flavors to match the many shapes, colors, and sizes available.

Serve with Eggplant Casserole (see page 197).

Scallops with Sesame Seed Sauce

What You Need

1½ pounds fresh scallops

1 garlic clove

½ cup plain pepitas

3 tablespoons sesame seeds

2 tablespoons vegetable oil

¾ teaspoon chili powder

¼ teaspoon cinnamon

⅛ teaspoon ground cloves

¾ cup chicken stock (see Chicken Stock, page 124)

½ teaspoon salt

1½ tablespoons lime juice

What You Do

1. Put scallops in a saucepan. Add ½" water. Cover and heat on low until scallops are opaque and firm.

2. Peel garlic. Combine pepitas, sesame seeds, garlic, and oil in a saucepan. Stir and cook over medium heat until sesame seeds are light golden brown.

3. Remove from heat and stir in chili powder, cinnamon, and ground cloves. Put sauce in an electric blender or food processor and grind. Add broth and salt. Grind again.

4. Turn mixture into a saucepan. Mix in lime juice and heat over low heat, stirring until thickened. Arrange scallops on a platter and spoon sauce over them.

?

What's Authentic Mexican Food?

Mexico is a big country with many different regions differentiated by climate, terrain, and indigenous culture. The food of the desert areas is not identical to that of the coastal regions, the beef-growing plains, or the tropical jungle areas. As in the United States, there are regional specialties, most of which can't be found in Mexican restaurants in the United States because the owners know that *Norteamericanos* won't recognize many of their finest dishes as truly Mexican.

LEVEL **M**

SERVINGS **4**

Shrimp in Prickly Pear Vinaigrette

Serve this with
Pineapple Coconut
Salad
(see page 94).

What You Need

2 prickly pear cactus fruits

1 bunch cilantro

½ cup red wine vinegar

2 tablespoons garlic paste

1 tablespoon peanut oil

28 cooked frozen large shrimp, thawed

1 tablespoon olive oil

½ tablespoon balsamic vinegar

1 (1-ounce) package hearts of palm

1 (6-ounce) package arugula

1 teaspoon salt

1 teaspoon ground black pepper

What You Do

1. Peel prickly pear cactus fruits by cutting off both ends and slitting both sides. If ripe, the peel will easily come off. Cut into 1" pieces. Cut stems off cilantro.

2. In a blender, combine cilantro, prickly pear cactus fruit, red wine vinegar, garlic paste, and peanut oil. Blend at medium speed until smooth.

3. Place shrimp in a glass or plastic container and pour sauce over the top. Cover and refrigerate for 8–12 hours. Discard sauce.

4. Preheat grill to medium temperature. Lay shrimp on grill and cook 2 to 3 minutes on each side or until slightly browned.

5. While shrimp are cooking, combine olive oil and balsamic vinegar. Cut hearts of palm into ½" pieces. Combine olive oil and balsamic vinegar mixture with salt, pepper, hearts of palm, and arugula. Toss gently.

6. Spread hearts of palm and arugula onto serving platter and top with fresh-grilled shrimp.

This is traditionally served on a platter garnished with pimiento-stuffed green olives and parsley.

Plain white rice is the traditional accompaniment.

Christmas Codfish

What You Need

1 pound piece of salted codfish

2 small yellow onions

2 garlic cloves

3 canned pimientos

3 medium red tomatoes

1 teaspoon salt

1 teaspoon black pepper

3 tablespoons vegetable oil

5 pickled jalapeño peppers

What You Do

1. Soak codfish 6–8 hours in cold water. Change water several times.

2. Peel onions. Peel garlic cloves. Slice pimientos into ¼" strips. Peel tomatoes and cut into quarters.

3. Drain codfish and put into a saucepan. Add 1 onion and water to cover. Bring to a simmer. Cover and cook gently about 15 minutes or until fish flakes easily when tested with a fork. Drain. Sprinkle salt and pepper on top.

4. While fish is cooking, put tomatoes, remaining onion, and garlic in an electric blender or food processor. Blend until puréed.

5. Heat oil in a skillet over medium heat. Add tomato purée. Cook until thickened, stirring occasionally. Mix in jalapeño peppers and pimiento strips.

Peppers or Peppercorns?

Chili peppers are not related at all to the plant that produces peppercorns. It's likely that they received the same name when the Spanish conquistadors arrived in Mexico during the 1500s and found that the chilies had a "bite" similar to the more familiar peppercorns.

LEVEL M

SERVINGS 4

Serve with Red Rice
(see page 212), and
Spinach Salad (see
page 89).

Flounder from Ixtapa

What You Need

1 small yellow onion

1 pound fresh flounder fillets

½ cup orange juice

1 cup canned tomato paste

1 cup water

1 teaspoon chili powder

1 teaspoon salt

½ teaspoon ground pepper

What You Do

1. Peel onion and chop into ¼" pieces.

2. Place fish fillets in a medium-sized frying pan and add water to cover. Add ¼ cup orange juice. Bring to a boil, reduce heat, and simmer about 10 minutes or until fish flakes when tested with a fork. Drain and skin, if necessary.

3. Cut fish into finger-sized pieces and return to frying pan.

4. In a small saucepan, combine ¼ cup orange juice, tomato paste, 1 cup water, onion, and chili powder. Bring to a boil. Add salt and pepper.

5. Pour sauce over fish fingers. Simmer fish uncovered until sauce thickens and fish is well coated.

Serve with Peppery
Mango Salad (see
page 95).

Baja-Style Crab

What You Need

1 cup dry white rice

1 pound crab meat

1 medium white onion

2 garlic cloves

2 fresh pimientos

2 medium tomatoes

2 medium carrots

¼ cup olive oil

1 teaspoon ground
annatto

2½ cups chicken stock
(see Chicken Stock, page
124)

1 teaspoon salt

½ teaspoon ground white
pepper

¼ cup dry sherry

What You Do

1. Preheat oven to 350°F. Soak the rice in hot water
   for 30 minutes. Break the crabmeat into 1" pieces.
   Peel onion and chop into quarters. Peel garlic and
   chop into quarters. Chop pimientos into quarters.
   Remove stems and peel tomatoes; chop into quarters. Peel carrots and slice into ¼" rounds.

2. Drain rice and place on paper towels to dry. Heat
   olive oil in a medium-sized frying pan to medium
   temperature. Cook rice until it is golden brown.

3. Put onion, garlic, tomatoes, annatto, and ½ cup of
   chicken stock in a blender or food processor. Blend
   on medium setting until smooth. Pour mixture into
   a mixing bowl.

4. Add 2 cups of chicken stock, rice, salt and pepper,
   the crab meat, pimientos, and carrots. Mix well and
   pour into an ovenproof casserole. Bake for 30 minutes. Gently stir in sherry and heat in oven an additional 5 minutes.

Fried Flounder with Green Sauce

This will please those who love spicy dishes!

Try adding some freshly grated Parmesan cheese on top of the fish filets during the last 10 minutes of baking for an additional flavor treat.

What You Need

4 flounder fillets (6–10 ounces each)

1 cup flour

3 tablespoons vegetable oil

½ small white onion

2 garlic cloves

8 fresh chili peppers, your choice

6 canned tomatillos, drained

¼ teaspoon ground cloves

½ teaspoon cinnamon

½ teaspoon nutmeg

½ teaspoon oregano

½ teaspoon cumin

½ teaspoon thyme

½ teaspoon rosemary

1 teaspoon parsley flakes

¼ cup lime juice

What You Do

1. Wash fillets with warm water and cover with flour.

2. Heat oil in a large frying pan on the stove to medium-high heat. Add fillets and fry on both sides until golden brown. Drain oil and place fillets in a baking dish.

3. Remove skin from onion and garlic. Remove stems and seeds from chili peppers. Cut tomatillos into quarters.

4. Preheat oven to 350°F.

5. Place garlic, onion, cloves, cinnamon, nutmeg, oregano, cumin, thyme, rosemary, parsley flakes, tomatillos, and lime juice in a food processor or blender. Blend at medium speed until you have a smooth purée.

6. Pour sauce over fish. Place fish in the oven and bake for 1 hour or until fish flakes easily with a fork.

This is best served with plain white rice or pinto beans.

It also goes well with fresh fruit.

Garlicky Seafood Sauté

What You Need

½ pound medium fresh shrimp

½ pound fresh lobster tail

½ pound fresh squid, cleaned

½ pound fresh scallops

4 medium tomatoes

16 garlic cloves

2 medium carrots

1 medium white onion

½ pound fresh spinach

½ cup vegetable oil

½ teaspoon white ground pepper

1 bunch fresh cilantro (parsley may be substituted for a milder flavor

What You Do

1. Preheat oven to 300°F.

2. Remove shells from shrimp and lobster tail. Place all seafood in a large pot of boiling water for 10 minutes. Drain and rinse with cold water. Cut squid into 1" lengths. Devein shrimp by running a fork tine along the back of each shrimp to remove the black-colored membrane. Cut the lobster tail into ½" pieces.

3. Cut tomatoes into ½" pieces. Remove skin from garlic and mince. Clean the carrots and cut into ¼" rounds. Remove the skin from the onion and chop into ¼" pieces. Remove the stems from the spinach. Cut cilantro into 1" pieces.

Garlicky Seafood Sauté—*continued*

4. Put the oil in a large frying pan and heat to medium. Add the onions and garlic. Cook until the onion is limp but not brown. The garlic should be light brown by this time. Drain oil and discard.

5. Lay the seafood in a 9" × 9" baking pan. Cover with garlic and onion mixture. Place in oven for 20 minutes.

6. While the seafood is in the oven, place spinach, tomatoes, and carrots into a vegetable steamer and cook until the spinach has wilted and the carrots are tender, about 10 minutes. (If you don't have a vegetable steamer, put 1" of water in the bottom of the pan and simmer the vegetables until tender.)

7. Right before serving, mix the steamed vegetables together and spread a layer on each plate. Lay a scoop of the seafood on top. Sprinkle with pepper and cilantro.

How Do I Thoroughly Clean Shrimp?

After you've boiled a shrimp and taken off its shell, look at the back and you will see a large vein running up the middle of the back. This is the equivalent of the shrimp's intestines. If you don't remove this membrane, you will be eating shrimp poop!

Seafood Paella

Enjoy this with fresh fruit and Spinach Salad (see page 89).

What You Need

1 small rock lobster tail	1 cup whole pimientos
24 fresh clams in shells	1 cup olive oil
1½ pounds shrimp	1½ teaspoons salt
1 pound scallops	2 cups uncooked rice
1 pound fresh crab meat	1 quart hot water
1 small yellow onion	1 cup fresh or frozen green peas
2 garlic cloves	¼ cup parsley
2 medium ripe tomatoes	

What You Do

1. Boil lobster, clams, shrimp, scallops, and crab about 10 minutes. Remove shells. Devein shrimp. Peel onion and mince. Peel garlic and mince. Remove stems from tomatoes and chop into ¼" pieces. Thaw peas if using frozen. Cut lobster into 1" cubes. Cut crab meat into 1" pieces. Cut pimientos into ¼"-wide strips.

2. Heat oil in a large frying pan. Add onion and garlic. Cook until onion is limp, about 2 minutes. Add tomatoes, salt, shrimp, clams, and scallops.

3. Add rice, 1 quart hot water, peas, and parsley. Mix well. Cover and cook, stirring occasionally, about 20 minutes or until rice is tender.

4. Mix in lobster, half of pimiento, and clams. Heat until very hot. Serve garnished with remaining pimiento.

Chapter 8
Vegetables

Serve with Mexican Pot Roast (see page 103).

Jalapeño Corn Bread

What You Need

1 small yellow onion

½ cup Cheddar cheese

1½ cups bread flour

¾ cup yellow cornmeal

¼ cup sugar

4½ teaspoons baking powder

1 teaspoon salt

1 egg

1 cup whole milk

½ teaspoon vegetable oil

½ cup canned cream-style corn

2 tablespoons canned chopped jalapeños, drained

½ teaspoon garlic paste

What You Do

1. Preheat oven to 350°F.

2. Remove skin from onion and chop into ¼" pieces. Grate Cheddar cheese.

3. Mix all ingredients together in a medium-sized mixing bowl.

4. Grease a bread pan and pour in mixture. Bake for 30–45 minutes or until lightly brown on top.

How Do I Know When Bread is Done Baking?

Bread that is fully cooked will spring back when you lightly touch the top with your finger. In addition, a toothpick inserted into the bread should come out clean. Most breads also will be lightly browned on top when they are done.

Use as the main
course for a summer
luncheon or serve
as the salad course
for a large dinner.

Vegetable-Stuffed Avocados v

What You Need

1 head cauliflower

¼ cup canned pimiento

2 tablespoons red wine vinegar

1½ teaspoons sugar

¼ teaspoon salt

⅓ cup vegetable oil

1 cup drained canned green peas

½ cup sliced black olives

3 large ripe avocados

What You Do

1. Cut cauliflower florets about the size of a dime until you have about 2 cups full. Chop pimiento into ¼" pieces.

2. Combine red wine vinegar, sugar, salt, and vegetable oil in a small container with a cover. Shake until well mixed.

3. Combine cauliflower florets, peas, black olives, and pimiento in a medium bowl. Cover with vinegar and oil dressing. Mix well. Cover and refrigerate 4–6 hours.

4. Peel, halve, and remove pits from avocados. Fill with cauliflower salad.

This is excellent served with a mild meat or fish dish.

Zucchini with Jalapeños v

What You Need

4 medium zucchini (8"–10" long)

2 medium tomatoes

1 medium yellow onion

2 garlic cloves

1 small green bell pepper

4 canned or fresh jalapeño peppers

½ teaspoon salt

½ teaspoon ground black pepper

1 tablespoon butter

What You Do

1. Chop zucchini and tomatoes into 1" pieces.

2. Remove skins from onions and garlic and chop into ¼" pieces.

3. Remove stem and seeds from bell pepper and jalapeños and chop into ¼" pieces.

4. Add all ingredients into medium-sized frying pan and cook on medium heat until the zucchini is tender but not limp.

Serve as the salad course to complement a spicy beef or pork dish.

Tomatoes with Guacamole v

What You Need

1 ripe avocado

2 garlic cloves

1 small yellow onion

4 large ripe tomatoes

2 tablespoons lime juice

1 teaspoon chili powder

4 tablespoons mayonnaise

1 cup whipping cream

½ teaspoon salt

½ teaspoon ground black pepper

16 fresh cilantro sprigs

What You Do

1. Peel avocado and remove pit. Peel garlic cloves and onion. Cut into quarters.

2. Slice tomatoes ¼" thick.

3. Put avocado, lime juice, chili powder, garlic, onion, mayonnaise, whipping cream, salt, and black pepper into a food processor or blender. Blend on medium until smooth.

4. Pour sauce over tomatoes and garnish with cilantro sprigs.

?

How Popular is Oregano in Mexican Cooking?

Oregano is one of the most common herbs found in the Mexican kitchen. It comes in many different varieties, although we usually see just one fresh variety in the United States. Unlike many spices, Mexicans will use dried oregano even when fresh is available.

Green Beans with Pine Nuts   v

This makes a wonderful pot-luck dish or a tame counterpart to a spicy beef dish.

You can substitute ¼ cup dried spearmint if fresh is unavailable.

What You Need

1½ pounds green beans

½ cup fresh spearmint leaves, packed

1 garlic clove

1 large red onion

1 cup pine nuts

¾ cup olive oil

¼ cup white vinegar

¾ teaspoon salt

½ teaspoon ground black pepper

1 cup crumbled feta cheese

What You Do

1. Wash green beans in cold water. Remove stems and cut in half. Bring 4 quarts water to boil in a large saucepan on medium-high heat. Add green beans and cook about 4 minutes or until tender but still crisp. Drain and immerse in ice-cold water for 2 minutes. Remove and spread on paper towels to dry.

2. Remove stems from spearmint and finely chop leaves into pieces about 1/16" square. Remove peel from garlic. Remove peel from onion and dice into pieces about ¼" square. Chop pine nuts into pieces about ¼" square.

3. Combine mint, oil, vinegar, salt, pepper, and garlic in a food processor or blender. Blend into ingredients are melded together. Cover and refrigerate for at least 2 hours.

4. Pat beans to remove any remaining water. Place beans in a serving bowl. Sprinkle pine nuts and onions and top with crumbled feta cheese. Pour dressing over the top and toss gently.

If you prefer mashed yams, don't bother layering the ingredients but combine everything and then mash the yams and mango right before serving.

Spiced Yams v

What You Need

4 medium-sized fresh yams

1 fresh ripe mango

½ cup honey

½ cup unflavored yogurt

1 tablespoon cinnamon

1 tablespoon butter

What You Do

1. Preheat oven to 350°F.

2. Peel yams and cut into ¼" thick rounds. Remove peel and seed from mango. Cut mango into ¼" slices.

3. Mix honey, yogurt, and cinnamon.

4. Grease a medium-sized, covered baking dish with butter. Layer half the yams then the mangos then the remaining half of the yams in the dish. Cover with the sauce.

5. Cover and place in the oven for 1 hour. Remove cover and place back in the oven for 30 minutes.

6. Drain remaining liquid from the pan before moving the yams and mango to a serving dish. Lightly toss before serving.

Are Yams or Sweet Potatoes the Same Thing?

Many people think yams and sweet potatoes are the same thing but they are definitely different. Sweet potatoes are shaped more like a potato and have a brighter, orange flesh. Yams are more elongated and have stringy hairs on their skin. Their flesh is more pale and less sweet.

Jalapeño Mashed Potatoes   v

You can try almost any peppers in this recipe to complement the main dish being served.

What You Need

4 medium potatoes

2 fresh jalapeño peppers

1 teaspoon salt

½ cup plain yogurt

1 teaspoon ground white pepper

1 teaspoon fresh epazote

1 tablespoon butter

What You Do

1. Place 1 quart of water in a large cooking pot and bring to a boil on medium-high heat.

2. Peel potatoes and cut into 1" cubes.

3. Remove stem and seeds from jalapeño peppers and cut into ¼" pieces.

4. Place potatoes, jalapeño peppers, and salt in water and boil about 15 minutes or until potatoes are easily pierced with a fork. Drain potatoes.

5. Combine yogurt, white pepper, and epazote in a small mixing bowl. Add to the potatoes and jalapeño peppers. Mash with a potato masher or hand mixer on low speed.

What's Epazote?

Epazote is a very common weed used as an herb in Mexican dishes. It has a very strong flavor, so it is frequently used to bring new flavor to common foods such as black beans, mushrooms, or squash. Only use the leaves as the stems are very tough and bitter. Dried epazote is available, though its flavor is not as strong due to the drying process.

This is a fun dish to serve with a milder seafood dish. The flavors offset each other very well.

Peppered Corn v

What You Need

2 (10-ounce) cans whole kernel sweet corn

2 poblano chilies

1 ancho chili

2 serrano chilies

1 small white onion

1 tablespoon dried cilantro

2 tablespoons butter

1 teaspoon ground black pepper

What You Do

1. Pour corn into a medium-sized pan and place on medium-low heat.

2. Remove stems and seeds from chilies and cut into ¼" pieces.

3. Remove skin from onion and cut into ¼" pieces.

4. Add chilies and onion to corn and cook until well heated.

5. Remove from stove and drain the liquid. Add the cilantro, butter, and black pepper. Mix well, making sure butter is melted.

Try this as a
surprising treat at
your next outdoor
barbecue.

Grilled Corn on the Cob v

What You Need

8 ears of fresh sweet corn

4 tablespoons butter

1 tablespoon cayenne pepper

1 teaspoon ground black pepper

1 teaspoon onion salt

1 teaspoon dried cilantro

What You Do

1. Preheat grill to medium temperature.

2. Peel back corn husks and remove hairs, leaving husks attached.

3. Mix butter, cayenne pepper, black pepper, onion salt, and cilantro together.

4. Use mixture to coat the corn.

5. Fold the husks back up onto the corn cob.

6. Place on grill, turning frequently. Check every few minutes to make sure the corn is not burning. The corn is done when a few kernels on each cob begin to turn light brown.

Virtually any green works well in this recipe.

If you live in a chemical-free area, try using dandelion leaves.

Mashed Chard v

What You Need

1 bunch chard leaves

1 small white onion

½ cup water

2 tablespoons butter

½ cup sour cream

1 teaspoon salt

1 tablespoon dried oregano

1 teaspoon ground black pepper

What You Do

1. Remove stems from chard and wash leaves thoroughly. Do not dry.

2. Remove skin from onion and cut into ¼" pieces.

3. Put chard and onion in a medium pot on the stove on low heat. Add ½ cup water.

4. Cook about 15 minutes or until chard is very limp.

5. Drain water. Add butter, sour cream, salt, oregano, and black pepper to pot. Mash with a potato masher.

Broccoli with Goat Cheese   v

Serve as a salad before a heavier dish such as Pork Roast with Apples (see page 118).

What You Need

½ cup fresh, packed chives

1 garlic clove

1 large red onion

1 cup chopped walnuts

1 cup crumbled goat cheese

¾ cup olive oil

¼ cup white vinegar

¾ teaspoon salt

¼ teaspoon ground black pepper

1½ pounds frozen broccoli, thawed

What You Do

1. Wash chives and cut into 2" lengths. Peel garlic. Peel onion and cut into ¼" pieces. Chop walnuts into small pieces and crumble goat cheese, if necessary.

2. Combine chives, oil, vinegar, salt, pepper, and garlic in a food processor and blend until smooth. Place in a bowl, cover, and refrigerate for at least 4 hours.

3. Place broccoli in a serving bowl. Sprinkle with nuts, cheese, and onions.

4. Just before serving, pour dressing over the broccoli and toss.

? What Kind of Cutting Board Should I Use?

Although many chefs prefer wooden cutting boards, plastic is actually more sanitary. Meat and vegetable juice can soak into wood, allowing bacteria to grow.

LEVEL **E**

SERVINGS **6**

This dish often is served as a side dish for meals such as Cinnamon Fried Chicken (see page 134).

Pastel de Elote (Corn Pie) v

What You Need

1 tablespoon shortening

1 (4-ounce) package Monterey jack cheese

1 (4-ounce) package sharp Cheddar cheese

½ cup butter

3 large eggs

1 can cream-style corn

1½ cups frozen corn, thawed

½ cup cornmeal

1 cup sour cream

½ cup canned chopped jalapeños, drained

½ teaspoon salt

¼ teaspoon Worcestershire sauce

What You Do

1. Preheat oven to 350°F.

2. Grease a pie plate with shortening. Cut cheeses into ½" cubes. Melt butter over low heat or in microwave.

3. In a large mixing bowl, beat eggs until frothy.

4. Add remaining ingredients. Stir until thoroughly mixed. Pour into pie plate.

5. Bake for 20 minutes.

?

What is an Easy Way to Glaze Vegetables?

For a quick and easy glaze for fresh vegetables, use equal parts brown sugar and honey. Add a pinch of salt and some grated orange peel.

Serve as a side dish to Salpicon (see page 105).

Calabacitas ᵥ

What You Need

3 small zucchini

1 large red tomato

2 fresh jalapeño peppers

1 garlic clove

½ pound mild Cheddar cheese

2 cups canned whole kernel corn

What You Do

1. Cut zucchini into 1" chunks. Chop tomatoes into ¼" pieces. Remove stems and seeds from jalapeño peppers and chop into ¼" pieces. Peel garlic and chop finely. Cut cheese into ½" chunks.

2. Put zucchini, tomatoes, peppers, and garlic into a large saucepan. Turn heat to medium-low. Heat slowly until ingredients are hot.

3. Add corn and cheese. Cover and continue to cook until cheese is melted.

How Many Varieties of Squash Are There?

Red. Yellow. Orange. Summer. Butternut. Acorn. Winter. Spaghetti. And those are just a few. Squash may have more varieties available in an average grocery store than any other fresh produce. The reason is that it keeps well throughout the winter and can be grown in virtually any climate. Each variety has its unique flavor and texture but most react well to being baked or mashed with cheese and spices.

LEVEL **E**

SERVINGS **6**

This goes very well as a side dish for Pork Roast with Apples (see page 118).

Eggplant Casserole v

What You Need

1 medium eggplant

½ teaspoon garlic salt

½ cup canned jalapeño peppers

½ teaspoon cumin

2 cups canned tomato sauce

½ cup sour cream

1½ cups shredded Cheddar cheese

What You Do

1. Preheat oven to 350°F.

2. Remove stem from eggplant. Wash rind but do not peel. Slice into ½" thick rounds. Arrange rounds in a 9" × 9" lightly greased baking pan. Sprinkle with garlic salt.

3. Combine jalapeño peppers, cumin, tomato sauce, and sour cream. Mix well. Pour over eggplant rounds.

4. Layer cheese over the top of the eggplant.

5. Bake for 45–60 minutes or until cheese is melted and eggplant is soft.

What's Eggplant?

Eggplants are a relative of the tomato and pepper families. They come in many colors but all taste rather bland. Like tofu, they are used for their ability to pick up the flavors of spicy and other ingredients in a dish.

This mild dish is the perfect accompaniment for a spicier main course.

Tomatillos with Zucchini v

What You Need

3 medium zucchini (8"–10" long)

4 medium tomatillos (or ¾ cup canned tomatillos)

1 large yellow onion

2 tablespoons butter

½ teaspoon oregano

½ teaspoon salt

1 tablespoon water

¼ cup grated Parmesan cheese

What You Do

1. Wash and remove stem from zucchini but do not peel. Cut zucchini into thin slices. Remove skin from tomatillos and chop into ¼" pieces. If using canned, discard juice. Peel onion and chop into ¼" pieces.

2. Melt butter in a large frying pan at medium heat. Add onion and cook until limp, not brown.

3. Add tomatillos, zucchini, oregano, salt, and water. Stir well.

4. Cover, bring to a boil, then reduce heat. Cook until zucchini is tender but still slightly crisp, about 6 minutes.

5. Stir in cheese before serving.

LEVEL **E**

SERVINGS **8**

This is perfect served with Barbecued Pork Ribs (see page 119), or any other grilled meat.

Grilled Zucchini v

What You Need

4 medium zucchini

2 garlic cloves

1 fresh habanero pepper

1 teaspoon salt

½ cup olive oil

1 teaspoon oregano

1 teaspoon chili powder

½ teaspoon ground black pepper

What You Do

1. Preheat grill to medium heat.

2. Wash zucchini, remove stems, and slice in half lengthwise.

3. Peel garlic and mince. Remove stem and seeds from habanero pepper and mince.

4. Combine garlic, habanero pepper, salt, oil, oregano, chili powder, and black pepper in a small covered container. Shake until well mixed.

5. Place zucchini flesh side down on grill for 10 minutes. Then place flesh side up. Use the oil and spice sauce to baste zucchini as it cooks. Serve when zucchini is soft.

Do Mexicans Use Feta Cheese?

Yes, the Mexicans do use feta cheese (or its equivalent). It is very similar to many goat cheeses that have been used since ancient times. In addition, it complements many of their hot, spicy dishes very well so they have adopted this traditionally Greek cheese.

Mexican Stuffed Peppers v

Serve as the
vegetable course
with a mild-flavored
poultry dish.

What You Need

8 fresh, large poblano peppers

1 tablespoon olive oil

2–3 cups Refried Beans (see page 211)

¼ cup mild Cheddar cheese

What You Do

1. Preheat oven to 300°F.

2. Remove stems from peppers and cut in half length-wise. Remove seeds.

3. Brush cavities with olive oil.

4. Place enough Refried Beans in each cavity to fill to the top. Don't heap the beans over the top.

5. Grate cheese and sprinkle a small amount on top of each stuffed pepper.

6. Place on a cookie sheet or in a baking pan. Bake in oven for 30 minutes.

This is a wonderful first course for any chicken or red meat dish.

Pumpkin blossoms are available at Mexican food markets or from your grandmother's garden! You also can substitute squash flowers or use a combination of the two.

Pumpkin Blossom Soup v

What You Need

1 small white onion

1 pound pumpkin blossoms

¼ cup butter

8 cups chicken broth (see Chicken Stock, page 124)

3 sprigs fresh parsley

1 teaspoon salt

1 teaspoon ground white pepper

What You Do

1. Remove skin from onion and chop into ¼" pieces. Remove stems from pumpkin blossoms and chop roughly into 2" pieces.

2. Melt butter in a small frying pan at medium heat and cook onions until limp but not brown. Add blossoms and cook for 5 minutes.

3. Put chicken broth, salt, pepper, and parsley in a medium stock pot. Bring to a boil and reduce heat to medium. Add butter and blossoms, discarding extra butter. Stir gently and simmer for 10 minutes.

Add onions, hot peppers, pimiento, minced garlic, or even peas and carrots to the dough to create interesting alternatives.

Aztec Potatoes v

What You Need

1 cup masa harina

¼ cup warm water

1½ cups leftover mashed potatoes

1 egg

½ cup shredded Monterey jack cheese

1 teaspoon salt

1 cup vegetable oil

What You Do

Combine masa harina with warm water and mashed potatoes and mix well. Beat egg. Add egg, cheese, and salt to flour and potato mixture. Mix well and form into patties about ¾" thick. Heat vegetable oil to medium temperature in a large frying pan. Fry patties until golden brown on both sides.

Try topping this with a sprinkling of ground pistachio meats.

Cactus Paddles v

What You Need

2 pounds cactus paddles

1 small yellow onion

4 garlic cloves

1 teaspoon oregano

2 tablespoons butter

1 cup sour cream

What You Do

Clean cactus paddles and pat dry. Cut into 1" pieces. Remove skin from onion and cut into ¼" pieces. Remove skin from garlic and cut into thin slices. Melt butter in a skillet on low heat. Add the cactus pieces, onion, garlic, and oregano. Cook, stirring periodically until the onion is clear. Draining remaining butter. Stir in 1 cup sour cream.

Turnip & Mustard Leaf Rolls v

What You Need

1 bunch turnip leaves	2 tablespoons epazote
1 bunch mustard leaves	1 teaspoon salt
4 tablespoons butter	1 teaspoon black pepper

What You Do

Remove stems from turnip and mustard leaves and wash leaves thoroughly. Pat dry with a paper towel. Layer one turnip leaf then one mustard leaf. Add ½ teaspoon of butter in center of mustard leaf. Sprinkle with epazote, salt, and black pepper. Roll up leaves. Place leaf rolls in a frying pan with a small amount of water. Cover and turn heat on low. Cook for 10 minutes on low heat.

Nut–Stuffed Chayote v

What You Need

2 chayote squash	¼ cup pecans
1 cup fresh mushrooms	¼ cup roasted almonds
¼ cup pistachio meats	½ cup honey

What You Do

Preheat oven to 350°F. Cut squash in half and remove seeds. Poke holes in the squash meat with a fork. Do not pierce the rind. Wash mushrooms and cut into quarters. Combine pistachios, pecans, and almonds. Grind in a food processor or nut grinder until you have small pieces. Combine nuts, mushrooms, and honey. Mix well and add ¼ to the cavity of each squash half. Place squash directly on oven rack. Bake for 1 to 2 hours or until squash is easily pierced with a fork.

To serve, pour sauce on a plate and top with the chili rellenos.

Add sides of Red Rice (see page 212), and Fresh Cauliflower Salad (see page 85).

Chili Rellenos en Croute v

What You Need

4 fresh poblano chili peppers

1 (8-ounce) package goat cheese

1 (12-ounce) package shredded Monterey jack cheese

2 sticks butter

1 box whole wheat phyllo pastry

16 Roma tomatoes

4 bunches fresh cilantro

½ cup chopped onion

1 tablespoon olive oil

1 teaspoon salt

What You Do

1. Preheat oven to 350°F. Put peppers on a cookie sheet and roast about 20 minutes or until well browned. Remove skin, stem, and seeds when cool. Do not cut pepper open other than at top.

2. Crumble goat cheese. Combine cheeses. Fill each pepper with ¼ of cheese mixture.

3. Melt butter in a small saucepan on low heat. Remove phyllo and lay out flat on a work surface. (Keep unused sheets of phyllo covered with damp towel.) Take 1 sheet of phyllo at a time and brush with butter, using a pastry brush. Put 1 chili in the corner of phyllo sheet and roll up, brushing all unbuttered surfaces with butter.

4. Place chili rellenos on a cookie sheet and bake at 350°F for 20 to 25 minutes or until dough is well-browned.

5. Cut tomatoes into ¼" pieces. Remove stems from cilantro and chop into ¼" pieces. Cook onion in olive oil at medium heat until onions are clear and limp. Add tomatoes and cook 5 to 10 minutes or until liquid is evaporated. Add salt and chopped cilantro. Stir well.

Stuffed Chayote Squash

While most Europeans tend to keep their fruit and vegetables separate, Mexicans make no distinction.

This dessert offers a unique blend of flavors to complement any Mexican meal.

What You Need

½ vanilla pound cake

3 chayote squash

3 eggs

1 cup golden raisins

1 cup sugar

1 teaspoon nutmeg

1 teaspoon cinnamon

1 cup dry white wine

½ cup crushed saltine crackers

½ cup toasted whole almonds

What You Do

1. Preheat oven to 350°F. Crumble pound cake.

2. Cut the chayotes in half and place in a large stock pot. Cover with water and bring to a boil. Reduce heat to medium and simmer for 15–20 minutes or until they are tender when pricked with a fork. Remove from water to cool.

3. When cool, remove the seeds and discard. Remove the pulp, leaving the shell intact. Mash the pulp.

4. Beat the eggs well. Combine with the pulp and mix well. Add raisins, sugar, nutmeg, cinnamon, white wine, crackers, and pound cake.

5. Stuff the chayote shells with the mixture. Press almonds into the top. Place in a greased, ovenproof casserole. Bake for 15 minutes.

What's a Chayote?

Chayote is actually a fruit but is most often used as a vegetable. It is a member of the squash family that is very popular in warm climates. It has a single seed that is edible and considered a delicacy.

Serve on a buffet
with traditional
Mexican favorites.

Coliflor Acapulco v

What You Need

1 large head fresh cauliflower

1½ cups vegetable oil

½ cup lemon juice

1½ teaspoon salt

1 teaspoon chili powder

¼ cup canned pimientos

2 cups canned pickled beets

1 large cucumber

8 red radishes

2 cups canned garbanzos, drained

1 cup pimiento-stuffed olives

1 cup lettuce

1 bunch parsley sprigs

1 cup Guacamole (see page 16)

What You Do

1. Add water to a large saucepan to the depth of 1".
   Bring water to a boil. Add cauliflower, cover, and
   cook about 20 minutes or until tender. Drain water.

2. Combine vegetable oil, lemon juice, salt, and chili
   powder in a covered container. Shake until well
   mixed to create a marinade.

3. Place cauliflower head down in a deep bowl and
   pour marinade over it. Cover and chill at least 8
   hours in the refrigerator.

Coliflor Acapulco—continued

4. Slice pimientos into ¼"-wide lengthwise strips. Slice pickled beets into ¼"-thick rounds. Slice cucumber into ¼" rounds. Chill these vegetables separately for at least 2 hours covered in the refrigerator.

5. Cut tops and bottoms off radishes and slice slightly down the sides to create roses.

6. Thread garbanzos, olives, and pimiento strips onto wooden picks to create decorative kabobs.

7. Drain cauliflower. Line a chilled serving plate with lettuce and place cauliflower, head up, in the center. Arrange pickled beets and cucumber slices around the base. Tuck in parsley sprigs and radish roses.

8. Spoon and spread guacamole over cauliflower. Decorate cauliflower with kabobs. Serve cold.

What's the Origin of Coliflor Acapulco?

Acapulco has been a resort community almost from the day Ponce de Leon first landed there. It is not as popular with Americans because it is an old, dirty port town and the bay is very polluted. However, it is still a popular resort community for Mexicans. It's likely this dish has been used to decorate fiesta tables for hundreds of years.

Green Mountain Stew

What You Need

1 pound mutton

1 pound skinless boneless chicken breasts

6 tomatillos

2 yellow onions

2 chayote squash

12 fresh serrano chilies

1 tablespoon vegetable oil

¾ teaspoon garlic paste

1 teaspoon salt

1 teaspoon ground black pepper

What You Do

1. Cut mutton and chicken into 1" cubes. Remove skin and stems from tomatillos and quarter. Peel onions and quarter. Remove rind and seed from chayote squash and cut flesh into 1" pieces. Remove stems from chilies and split in half lengthwise.

2. Heat vegetable oil to medium temperature in a large frying pan. Add mutton and chicken meat. Fry until meat is golden. Add tomatillos, garlic, squash, onion, chilies, salt, and pepper. Mix lightly. Fry for 5 minutes. Reduce heat to medium-low. Cover and simmer for 1½ hours.

? What are Jalapeño Peppers?

Jalapeños are perhaps the most common hot pepper sold in the United States. They come in both green and red colors that taste only slightly different. When in doubt, use jalapeños because they definitely add heat and spice but they are mild enough that most people can tolerate them.

Chapter 9

Rice and Beans Dishes

LEVEL **E**

SERVINGS *

*This recipe yields 3 cups.

This is the foundation of many Mexican dishes. Multiply the proportions of 1 part rice to 2 parts liquid to get larger amounts, and divide for smaller. Be sure to keep the two elements in proportion.

Basic Cooked Rice   v

What You Need

1 cup uncooked rice

2 cups liquid (water, broth, etc.)

What You Do

1. Put rice and liquid in a pot and bring to a boil.

2. Reduce heat to low and cover tightly.

3. Simmer for 20 minutes. Stir with a fork before serving or using.

LEVEL **E**

SERVINGS *

*This recipe yields 3 to 4 cups.

You can always use the old method of soaking beans overnight, but this quick method works just as well.

Beans are a wonderful slow-cooker food.

The slow cooker gives them the steady, low heat they need to cook up beautifully tender.

Quick & Easy Beans   v

What You Need

2 cups dry beans (pinto, black, or any kind you like)

4 cups water (you can use broth for a meatier taste if you prefer)

What You Do

1. Put beans and water into a large pot and bring to a boil.

2. Turn off burner and leave pan with lid on for an hour.

3. Turn heat on low and simmer for 2–4 hours until tender, depending on type of bean. (Some beans, like kidney or garbanzo, take longer.)

LEVEL **E**

SERVINGS **8**

This is a basic recipe used in many other recipes in this book.

You can also use Refried Beans instead of ground beef, pulled beef, or pulled chicken in any recipe.

Add chili powder or diced chilies if you want a little spice in your beans.

If you use oil rather than lard to cook these, this will be a vegetarian dish.

Refried Beans v

What You Need

1 large white onion

½ cup lard or vegetable oil

¼ teaspoon garlic paste

1 teaspoon salt

1 teaspoon ground black pepper

2 15-ounce cans (or 4 cups cooked) pinto or black beans (or whatever kind of bean you choose)

What You Do

1. Remove skin from onion and chop into ¼" pieces.

2. Melt lard in large frying pan over medium heat. Add onion, garlic, salt, and pepper. Cook, stirring frequently, on medium heat until onion is tender and golden but not browned.

3. Mash beans with a potato masher. Add mashed beans to oil and onion mixture. Stir lightly to mix onion into beans.

4. Cook on medium heat until liquid evaporates.

What are Refried Beans?

Often in Mexico when you order Refried Beans you receive a bowl of warm beans and onions with a triangle of dry toast. In short, they don't have to be mashed to be refried. They also don't have to be pinto beans. Any bean that is cooked twice is considered refried.

Add some spice to this recipe by including ¼ cup of your favorite hot peppers chopped into small pieces.

Red Rice v

What You Need

2 medium red tomatoes

1 bunch fresh green onions or scallions

1 tablespoon vegetable oil

3 cups cooked white rice (see Basic Cooked Rice, page 210)

1 teaspoon salt

1 teaspoon ground black pepper

What You Do

1. Remove stems from tomatoes. Place in food processor and blend on medium setting for about 30 seconds.

2. Remove skins and roots from onions and chop into ¼" pieces.

3. Put oil in a large frying pan and heat to medium-high. Add all ingredients. Stir well.

4. Cover and simmer for 10 minutes.

Red, White, & Green Rice Salad   v

This salad in the colors of the Mexican flag makes an excellent vegetable or starch substitute for any summer meal.

It also is the perfect potluck pleaser.

What You Need

1 medium green bell pepper

2 medium tomatoes

3 green onions

2 hardboiled eggs

2 cups cooked rice

2 small pimientos, chopped

1 teaspoon marjoram

½ teaspoon basil

1 tablespoon parsley

¼ cup vegetable oil

¼ cup olive oil

¼ cup wine vinegar

1 teaspoon salt

What You Do

1. Remove stem and seeds from green bell pepper. Slice into ¼" strips. Cut tomatoes into ½" cubes. Remove skin and roots from green onions. Slice into ¼" pieces. Peel eggs and chop into ¼" pieces.

2. Combine rice, pepper, pimientos, tomatoes, green onions, and eggs in a medium-sized bowl. Toss until well mixed.

3. Chop marjoram, basil, and parsley into small pieces. Combine in a small bowl. Add vegetable oil, olive oil, vinegar, and salt. Stir well to create dressing.

4. Pour dressing over salad. Cover and chill for at least 1 hour before serving.

This is an excellent complement to a poultry or red meat dish.

Gordo v

What You Need

2 small yellow onions

1 garlic clove

3 cups cooked white rice (see Basic Cooked Rice, page 210)

1 cup sour cream

½ cup shredded Parmesan cheese

1½ cups shredded Cheddar cheese

½ cup green chili peppers

1 teaspoon salt

¼ teaspoon black pepper

What You Do

Preheat oven to 300°F. Remove skin from onions and garlic and chop into ¼" pieces. Mix ingredients by stirring them in a mixing bowl. Lightly butter or grease a square baking dish. Add mixture and bake covered for 35 minutes. Remove cover and bake an additional 5 minutes.

Serve as a side dish to any fish or chicken meal.

Jalapeño Rice v

What You Need

3 cups cooked white rice (see Basic Cooked Rice, page 210)

½ teaspoon salt

2 cups sour cream

1 (8-ounce) package shredded Monterey jack cheese

⅛ cup canned chopped green chilies

¼ cup butter

What You Do

Preheat oven to 350°F. Grease a 9" baking pan. Layer rice, salt, sour cream, cheese, and chilies in pan. Dot with butter on top. Bake in oven for about 30 minutes.

Serve with Mexican Pot Roast (see page 103).

Arroz con Queso v

What You Need

¼ cup canned, diced jalapeños, drained

1 pint sour cream

6 cups cooked rice

¾ pound shredded Monterey jack cheese

½ cup shredded Cheddar cheese

What You Do

1. Preheat oven to 350°F.

2. Mix jalapeños into the sour cream.

3. In a 1-quart casserole, layer ingredients in the following order: half the cooked rice, half the sour cream with jalapeños, half the Monterey jack cheese, half the cooked rice, half the sour cream with jalapeños, half the Monterey Jack cheese.

4. Bake for 30 minutes. Top with cheddar cheese and broil 2 to 3 minutes before serving.

Can Low-Fat Milk Products Be Used in Recipes?

Low-fat cheese and sour cream can be substituted in most recipes. However, they do not melt as well and do not hold up over a long heating time so they do not work well in appetizers and dips.

Serve with a crisp green salad and fresh fruit for a well-balanced meal.

Casa Grande Rice   v

What You Need

1 large yellow onion

2 tablespoons butter

1 cup frozen spinach, thawed and squeezed dry

¼ teaspoon garlic salt

4½ cups cooked rice

1½ cup shredded Colby cheese

4 eggs

½ cup milk

2 teaspoons salt

½ teaspoon ground black pepper

What You Do

1. Preheat oven to 350°F.

2. Peel onion and chop into ¼" pieces.

3. In a large frying pan, melt butter. Add onion and cook until clear and tender but not brown. Add spinach, garlic salt, rice, and cheese. Mix well.

4. Combine eggs, milk, salt, and pepper. Mix well. Stir into rice mixture.

5. Pour into a casserole and bake uncovered for 30 minutes.

Serve as a summer luncheon with fresh Flour Tortillas (see page 286), and Jasmine & Rose Hips Tea (see page 39).

Cold Rice & Beans v

What You Need

3 celery ribs

1 medium red onion

1 bunch fresh cilantro

4½ cups cooked rice

2 cups canned pinto beans, drained and rinsed

2 cups canned black beans, drained and rinsed

1 cup frozen peas, thawed

1 cup canned chopped jalapeño peppers, drained

2 tablespoons water

⅓ cup white wine vinegar

¼ cup olive oil

1 teaspoon salt

½ teaspoon garlic powder

½ teaspoon ground black pepper

¼ teaspoon cayenne pepper

What You Do

1. Cut celery ribs into ¼" pieces. Peel onion and cut into ¼" rounds. Remove stems from cilantro and chop leaves roughly into ½" pieces.

2. Combine rice, pinto beans, black beans, peas, celery, onion, jalapeño peppers, and cilantro in a large serving bowl. Toss lightly to mix.

3. In a small glass jar combine 2 tablespoons water, white wine vinegar, olive oil, salt, garlic powder, black pepper, and cayenne pepper. Cover and shake until well mixed. Pour over salad. Toss until all ingredients are covered. Cover and refrigerate for at least 24 hours before serving.

Rice with Sautéed Pork

Serve with Tropical Gelatin (see page 253), and fresh Flour Tortillas (see page 286).

What You Need

1 pound fresh pork

1 medium yellow onion

2 tablespoons olive oil

¼ teaspoon garlic powder

¾ cup canned tomato paste

2 teaspoons salt

½ teaspoon oregano

½ teaspoon ground cumin

1½ teaspoon chili powder

1 cup water

2 cups canned pinto beans, drained and rinsed

4½ cups cooked rice

What You Do

Cut pork into thin slices. Peel onion and cut into ¼" pieces. Heat oil to medium temperature in a large frying pan. Add pork and cook until browned. Add onions and garlic powder. Cook lightly until onions are soft and clear but not brown. Stir in tomato paste, salt, oregano, cumin, chili powder, and 1 cup water. Turn heat to low. Cover and simmer 30 minutes. Add beans. Stir lightly. Cover and simmer for 15 minutes longer. Stir in rice. Cook uncovered for 10 minutes.

How Can I Easily Slice Meat Thinly?

To easily cut meat into small cubes or strips, thaw it only partially then use a large kitchen knife and cut the meat as you would a brick of cheese. It should have about the same consistency.

Add one chopped pepper of your choice to the recipe to make a spicier version of this meal.

Arroz con Pollo

What You Need

1 medium onion

4 large tomatoes

2 teaspoons salt

1 large cut-up chicken

4 tablespoons shortening

1½ cup uncooked brown rice

¼ teaspoon garlic paste

1 teaspoon black pepper

1 teaspoon cumin seed

2–3 cups warm water

What You Do

1. Remove skin from onion and slice into ¼"-thick rings. Cut tomatoes into eighths. Sprinkle salt over chicken pieces.

2. Melt shortening in a large frying pan over medium heat. Add rice and stir constantly until rice is browned.

3. In a separate frying pan, brown chicken over medium heat. Place chicken pieces over top of rice. Add tomatoes, onion, garlic, spices, and 2 cups warm water. Cover and simmer over low heat until rice is tender and fluffy. If the mixture dries before the rice is cooked, add more warm water.

 What Types of Arroz Are There?

Arroz is simply the Spanish word for rice. As in most other warm-weather cultures around the world, the Mexicans have adopted rice as a staple of their diet. Although they usually use white rice in their cooking, brown rice is favored when seeking a heartier dish.

Serve with Pork
Roast with Apples
(see page 118).

Cumin Rice v

What You Need

2 tablespoons butter

1 medium chopped red bell pepper

⅔ cup frozen chopped green pepper, thawed

¼ cup chopped onion

¼ teaspoon garlic paste

1 teaspoon cumin

1½ cups uncooked white rice

1½ cups hot chicken stock (see Chicken Stock, page 124)

What You Do

1. Heat butter to medium temperature in a saucepan. Add red bell pepper, green peppers, and onion. Cook until onion is limp but not brown. Add garlic, cumin, rice, and hot chicken stock. Mix well and cover saucepan.

2. Bring to a boil, reduce heat, and cook about 20 minutes or until rice is tender and liquid is absorbed.

How Should I Store Spices?

Store ground spices, dried herbs, and seeds in airtight containers away from light. Keep spices away from all heat and humidity sources to retain their integrity.

This is traditionally served with tortillas or dry toast triangles.

However, it also makes an excellent meat substitute in tacos or enchiladas.

Extra Special Frijoles Refritos

What You Need

5 slices bacon

2 cloves garlic

⅔ cup chopped onion

4 large tomatoes

5½ cups cooked pinto beans, drained

1 teaspoon salt

1 teaspoon ground black pepper

1 teaspoon oregano

1 teaspoon cumin

What You Do

1. Fry bacon crisply in a large frying pan. Set bacon on a paper towel to drain grease. Chop roughly.

2. Remove skin from garlic and mince. Add onion and garlic to bacon grease and cook on medium heat until golden brown.

3. Cut tomatoes into ½" pieces. Add tomatoes and beans to onions and garlic in frying pan. Stir together. Add salt, pepper, oregano, and cumin. Mix thoroughly. Stir in chopped bacon.

Black Bean & Avocado Burritos v

Add diced chicken or shredded beef to the filling for a heartier meal.

Serve with tortilla chips and Chili con Queso (see page 14).

What You Need

4 flour tortillas (see Flour Tortillas, page 286)

1 medium avocado

1 cup cooked brown rice

1 cup fresh cooked or canned black beans

¼ cup chopped canned green chilies, drained

¼ cup canned or frozen corn, drained or thawed

½ cup chopped onion

2 tablespoons chopped fresh cilantro

¼ teaspoon. salt

½ teaspoon black pepper

½ cup shredded Monterey jack cheese

½ cup shredded lettuce

½ cup salsa

What You Do

1. Heat tortillas in ungreased skillet or placa.

2. Remove the skin and pit from the avocado and chop the avocado meat into ½" pieces.

3. Combine the rice, beans, green chilies, corn, onion, cilantro, salt, and pepper in a medium-sized bowl. Mix well.

4. Remove the tortillas and place ½ cup of the rice and bean mixture in the center of each tortilla. Top each with ¼ of the avocado, 2 tablespoons cheese, 2 tablespoons lettuce and 1 tablespoon salsa.

5. Roll up each tortilla. Fold over ends before serving.

? How Can I Make an Edible Soup Bowl?

Use squash as a soup bowl. Many small squashes make excellent complements to soups and stews. Cut them in half, remove the seeds and pre-bake in the microwave or oven. Ladle your soup or stew into the squash for a festive look.

Mixed Bean Salad v

For some added zing, add a chopped hot pepper to the salad and some cayenne pepper to the dressing.

What You Need

1 15-ounce can garbanzo beans, drained and rinsed

1 15-ounce can pinto beans, drained and rinsed

1 15-ounce can black beans, drained and rinsed

1 15-ounce can green beans, drained

1 medium red onion

2 garlic cloves

1 medium carrot

1 medium cucumber

1 cup vegetable oil

½ cup white vinegar

¼ cup lemon juice

1 teaspoon salt

1 teaspoon ground black pepper

½ cup roasted pecans

What You Do

1. Drain water from all beans and rinse with cold water. Combine in a large mixing bowl.

2. Remove skin from onion and cut into ¼" rounds. Remove skin from garlic and cut into thin slices. Peel carrot and cut into ¼" rounds. Peel cucumber and cut into ¼" rounds. Mix these ingredients with beans.

3. In a small covered container, mix the vegetable oil, vinegar, lemon juice, salt, and ground black pepper. Shake until well blended. Pour on the bean and vegetable mix. Toss gently until well mixed. Chill overnight before serving. Right before serving, sprinkle pecans on top.

Serve with fresh
tortillas sprinkled
with garlic salt.

Mixed Bean Soup

What You Need

1 cup each dried pinto,
kidney, and black beans

1 large carrot

1 fresh jalapeño or
habanero pepper

½ cup chopped onion

2 medium red tomatoes

½ teaspoons garlic paste

1 teaspoon chili powder

2 teaspoons salt

½ teaspoon red chili
pepper

2 cups chicken broth (see
Chicken Stock, page 124)

What You Do

1. Soak beans overnight in 6 cups water or use Quick
   & Easy Beans (see page 210) process to ready beans
   for cooking.

2. Peel carrot and chop into ¼" pieces. Remove stem
   and seeds from jalapeño pepper.

3. Add all ingredients except chicken broth to a large
   stock pot, leaving tomatoes whole. Bring to a boil
   for 5 minutes. Reduce heat to medium-low and
   simmer uncovered for 3 hours.

4. Drain water and put ingredients in a blender. (You
   may need to divide it into two or three groups.)
   Blend on medium setting for 2 minutes or until
   ingredients make a paste. Stir in chicken broth.
   Reheat to serving temperature.

Why is Blending so Popular in Mexican Cooking?

Mexicans love to use their blenders and mashers. While similar dishes
in other cultures leave the ingredients in chunky bites, the Mexican
versions often have them blended together to create a unique meld of
flavors.

Beer Beans

Serve as a side dish to Barbecued Pork Ribs (see page 119), or another meat dish.

What You Need

2 cups dark Mexican beer

5 cups cooked but still firm pinto beans, drained

2 pieces bacon

2 large red tomatoes

½ chopped onion

¾ teaspoon garlic paste

4 chopped pickled jalapeño peppers, drained

1 teaspoon salt

1 teaspoon ground black pepper

What You Do

1. Add beer to pinto beans in large pot. Stir and cook on low heat.

2. Fry bacon until very crisp. Reserve grease in frying pan. Put bacon on a paper towel to cool. When cool, crumble into pieces about ¼" square.

3. Remove stems from tomatoes and chop into ½" pieces.

4. Add the onion to the bacon grease. Cook until the onion is clear and limp. Add the tomato, garlic paste, and jalapeño peppers. Stir to blend. Cook about 5 minutes.

5. Add the tomato mixture to the beans. Stir in crumbled bacon, salt, and pepper. Bring to a boil, reduce heat to low, and simmer for about 15 minutes.

LEVEL **E**

SERVINGS **6**

Serve with fresh
Tostadas (see
page 287), and
Guacamole (see
page 16).

Bean Burritos   v

What You Need

2 teaspoons ground cumin

3 cups Refried Beans (see page 211)

¼ cup sour cream

1 cup tomato salsa (see Tomato Salsa, page 12)

6 large flour tortillas (see Flour Tortillas, page 286)

½ cup shredded Monterey jack cheese

What You Do

1. Place the cumin in a small frying pan on low heat. Heat until toasted and fragrant, stirring constantly.

2. Place the beans in a blender or food processor and blend on medium speed until smooth. Add cumin and sour cream. Blend until well mixed.

3. Remove from blender and stir in tomato salsa.

4. Add about ⅔ cup of mixture to the center of each tortilla. Sprinkle cheese on top. Fold over ends and roll up.

You can also add beef, chicken, or pork to these fried tacos.

They're wonderful served with guacamole and various salsas for dipping.

Enrollados ∨

What You Need

1 medium yellow onion

2 medium red tomatoes

3 cups Refried Beans (see page 211)

1 cup Red Chili Sauce (see page 17)

12 flour tortillas (see Flour Tortillas, page 286)

1 (6-ounce) package shredded Monterey jack cheese

2 eggs

½ cup flour

½ cup vegetable oil

What You Do

1. Peel onion and chop into ¼" pieces. Remove stems from tomatoes and chop into ¼" pieces.

2. Heat beans on low heat in a medium saucepan. Add Red Chili Sauce, onion, and tomatoes. Heat through.

3. In the center of each tortilla, put about ⅓ cup of the mixture. Add about 2 tablespoons of cheese. Roll up tortilla as you would an enchilada.

4. Heat oil to medium-high. Beat eggs in a medium bowl. Roll each tortilla in flour and then in the beaten eggs. Place in frying pan and fry in vegetable oil until golden brown on all sides.

Should I Use Canned or Fresh Peppers?

A stop at a local Wal-Mart in the northern states found no fewer than seven varieties of fresh chili peppers. As a result, you likely will be able to find some to meet your needs virtually anywhere. I've usually called for canned to make recipes easier, except in recipes where having fresh peppers is crucial for taste and texture. If you still must use canned in these recipes, plan to use about half as much as you would fresh, and if you choose to replace canned peppers in other recipes, plan on twice the amount.

Lima Bean Casserole

Serve with fresh fruit for a well-balanced meal.

What You Need

¼ pound spicy sausage

¼ pound ham

¼ cup vegetable oil

½ cup chopped onion

1 cup Red Chili Sauce (see page 17)

2 pounds frozen lima beans, thawed

½ cup shredded Monterey jack cheese

What You Do

1. Remove casing from sausage if necessary. Cut ham into ½" cubes.

2. Heat oil in a medium skillet over medium heat. Add onion and sausage. Cook until sausage is browned. Add ham and Red Chili Sauce. Cover and cook about 30 minutes.

3. Skim off excess fat. Add beans and continue cooking about 15 minutes longer.

4. Sprinkle with cheese before serving.

LEVEL **E**

SERVINGS **4**

Serve as a stew with fresh Flour Tortillas (see page 286).

Mexican Pork & Beans

What You Need

¼ pound sliced bacon

¼ pound boneless pork tenderloin

¼ pound ham

½ cup chopped onion

1½ cups canned diced tomatoes

1 teaspoon chili powder

½ teaspoon cumin

½ teaspoon oregano

2 cups canned pinto beans

1 cup tequila

What You Do

1. Cook bacon on medium heat in a frying pan until crisp. Set on paper towels to drain. When cool, crumble.

2. Brown pork and ham in bacon fat. Add onion. Turn heat to medium. Cover and cook until soft, about 5 minutes.

3. Add tomatoes, chili powder, cumin, oregano, and the crumbled bacon. Stir well. Add cooked beans. Bring to a boil. Gradually stir in tequila.

4. Continue to cook uncovered for 1 hour, or until pork is well done and mixture is the consistency of a rich stew. Stir occasionally.

Dry Soup?

Many Mexican dishes feature bread or tortillas that are soaked in a sauce until the dish resembles more of a casserole or heavy stew than a soup. In Mexico, they refer to these dishes as dry soups. Why? We're not sure, but it's an apt description.

This makes an excellent accompaniment to Citrus Veal (see page 104).

Garbanzos with Sausage

What You Need

½ pound pork sausage

⅓ cup chopped onion

¼ teaspoon garlic paste

1 teaspoon chili powder

2 cups canned garbanzo beans, drained and rinsed

½ cup canned sliced pimientos, drained

½ teaspoon salt

¼ teaspoon oregano

½ teaspoon ground black pepper

What You Do

1. Brown sausage in a frying pan on medium heat. Add onion, garlic, and chili powder. Cook until onion is soft.

2. Add garbanzo beans and pimientos. Stir well. Bring to a simmer. Add salt, oregano, and pepper and serve.

Rice & Chicken with Guacamole

Serve as a summer luncheon with Brie and Papaya Quesadillas (see page 30).

What You Need

1 tablespoon vegetable oil

4 skinless, boneless chicken breasts

1 medium yellow onion

3 celery ribs

4½ cups cooked rice

1 cup frozen peas, thawed

1 teaspoon salt

1 teaspoon black pepper

1 cup mayonnaise

1½ teaspoon Tabasco or other hot sauce

¼ cup diced canned pimientos, drained

1 large avocado

½ teaspoon Worcester-shire sauce

1 cup sour cream

½ teaspoon onion flakes

½ teaspoon garlic salt

½ teaspoon onion salt

What You Do

1. Bring vegetable oil to medium temperature in a medium-sized frying pan. Add chicken breasts and cook until meat is lightly browned on all sides. Cut breasts with a knife to make sure they are thoroughly cooked. Set on a paper towel to cool.

2. Cut chicken breasts into 1" cubes when cooled. Peel onion and cut into ½" pieces. Cut celery into ¼" pieces. In a large serving bowl, combine rice, chicken, peas, onion, celery, salt, black pepper, ½ cup mayonnaise, 1 teaspoon hot sauce, and pimientos. Toss lightly until well mixed.

4. Peel avocado and remove pit. Mash until no chunks remain. Combine avocado, remaining ½ cup mayonnaise, Worcestershire sauce, sour cream, onion flakes, garlic salt, onion salt, and remaining ½ teaspoon hot sauce. Mix well. Pour dressing over salad and mix until all ingredients are covered. Cover and refrigerate at least 4 hours before serving.

Serve as a side dish for Cinnamon Fried Chicken (see page 134).

Baked Green Rice v

What You Need

1 bunch parsley

1 bunch green onions

2 eggs

4½ cups cooked rice

2 cups shredded mild Cheddar cheese

⅓ cup butter

¼ cup canned chopped green chilies, drained

4 chopped canned tomatillos, drained

1 teaspoon salt

½ teaspoon ground black pepper

1 cup milk

What You Do

1. Preheat oven to 350°F.

2. Cut stems from parsley and chop into small pieces. Chop green onions and their stems into ¼" pieces. Beat eggs.

3. Combine hot rice with cheese and butter. Toss until well mixed. Add chilies, parsley, onions, tomatillos, salt, and pepper. Mix well. Add beaten eggs and milk. Stir well.

4. Turn into a greased 2-quart baking dish. Cover and bake 30 minutes. Uncover and bake an additional 10 minutes.

Sherried Raisin-Rice Pudding   v

Add whipped cream and coconut to each dish right before serving to create a festive atmosphere.

What You Need

⅔ cup golden raisins

¼ cup dry red sherry

1 egg

1 cup uncooked white rice

1 teaspoon grated lemon peel

½ teaspoon salt

1½ cups water

3 cups whole milk

1 cup sugar

½ teaspoon cinnamon

What You Do

1. Soak raisins in sherry for 15 minutes. Beat egg and set aside.

2. Put rice, lemon peel, salt, and water in a saucepan. Bring to a boil. Reduce heat to low, cover, and cook until all water is absorbed (about 15 minutes).

3. Stir in milk, sugar, and cinnamon and cook over very low heat, stirring frequently, until all milk has been absorbed.

4. Stir in soaked raisins then beaten egg. Continue to heat, stirring constantly, until the egg is cooked (about 1 to 2 minutes).

5. Turn pudding into a serving dish. Chill in refrigerator 2–3 hours before serving.

Serve with fried Chorizo (see page 107).

Creamed Rice with Chilies   v

What You Need

4 habanero chilies

2 tablespoons butter

½ cup chopped onion

½ teaspoon garlic paste

1 cup frozen peas, thawed

1 cup frozen kernels, thawed

2 cups sour cream

1 (8-ounce) package shredded Monterey jack cheese

6 cups cooked rice

What You Do

1. Remove stems and seeds from habanero chilies and cut into ¼" pieces.

2. Melt butter in a medium frying pan on medium heat. Add onions and garlic. Cook until onions are limp but not brown. Reduce heat to medium-low. Add peas and corn. Cook until thoroughly heated. Stir in sour cream and cheese. Cook, stirring often, until cheese is melted.

3. Add rice to vegetable and cheese mixture. Stir until well blended. Pour into an ovenproof casserole. Bake for 30 minutes or until it is slightly brown on top.

? ## What Makes a Salsa?

Salsa actually means sauce. It can be hot, cold, chunky, or runny. Except when you use it as a dip for chips, salsa invariably is used as a topping for a dish or as a basic ingredient to complement the other ingredients in a recipe.

LEVEL **H**

SERVINGS **6**

Serve as a side dish for Jalapeño Chicken (see page 133).

Bean-Stuffed Peppers ᵥ

What You Need

2 eggs

6 red bell peppers

3 cups Refried Beans (see page 211)

¼ cup flour

1 cup shortening

½ cup cream

¼ pound shredded Monterey jack cheese

What You Do

1. Preheat oven to 350°F. Separate eggs. Beat the egg yolks until thick. Beat the whites until they are shiny and stiff. Fold the egg whites into the egg yolks. Remove stems and seeds from red bell peppers. Stuff with Refried Beans. Dust the peppers with flour, then dip into the egg mixture.

2. Melt shortening in a medium frying pan. Put 2 or 3 peppers in the pan at a time and fry on all sides.

3. Arrange the peppers in an ovenproof casserole dish. Cover with cream and sprinkle with cheese. Bake about 20 minutes or until the beans are hot.

Serve with Jalapeño & Mango Cornbread (see page 238).

Bean-Stuffed Zucchini   v

What You Need

2 medium zucchini (about 10" long)

3 tablespoons butter or margarine

1 cup chopped onion

⅔ cup frozen chopped green bell pepper

2 teaspoons cumin

1 teaspoon basil

2 teaspoons Red Chili Sauce (see page 17)

2 cups Refried Beans (see page 211)

1 (8-ounce) package shredded Monterey jack cheese

¾ cup sour cream

What You Do

1. Preheat oven to 350°F.

2. Wash zucchini and slice off ends. Slice each zucchini lengthwise and scoop out centers. Place in a 9" × 12" baking pan. Chop the zucchini centers and set aside.

4. Melt butter in a large frying pan at medium heat. Add onion and green bell pepper. Cook until onion is clear and tender. Add cumin, basil, Red Chili Sauce, and zucchini centers. Cook an additional 5 minutes. Add beans. Stir well and cook another 5 minutes. Add the cheese. Stir and cook until cheese melts. Turn the heat off and stir in the sour cream.

5. Stuff the zucchini shells with the cooked mixture. Bake for 30 to 40 minutes or until mixture is hot and bubbly.

? What Kind of Dressing is Popular in Mexican Cooking?

Americans and most Europeans prefer an oily dressing, using about twice as much oil as vinegar. Mexicans, however, enjoy a stronger vinegar taste in their dressings. They also frequently add a bit of citrus juice, such as lime, to their dressing to give an added zing.

Chapter 10

Fruit

LEVEL **E**

SERVINGS **10**

Serve for breakfast to accompany Huevos Bogotano (see page 130).

Jalapeño & Mango Cornbread v

What You Need

1 tablespoon active dry yeast

¼ cup water

1 medium white onion

1 mango

3 cups cornmeal

½ cup vegetable oil

1½ cups shredded Cheddar cheese

1 cup canned cream-style corn

2 tablespoons sliced canned jalapeño pepper

3 tablespoons sugar

⅓ cup whole milk

⅓ cup buttermilk

What You Do

1. Preheat oven to 425°F.

2. Dissolve yeast in ¼ cup warm water. Peel onion and chop into ¼" pieces. Remove skin and seed from mango. Cut into ¼" pieces.

3. Combine all ingredients in a large mixing bowl. Mix until well blended.

4. Pour into a greased bread pan. Place in oven and bake for 35 minutes.

❓ What's Yeast?

Yeast is a live entity that grows when it gets warm. However, if it's added to boiling water, you can kill it. You can make a heavy, dense bread by leaving out the yeast and substituting baking soda.

Fruit Tacos v

What You Need

2 ripe bananas

1 medium sweet apple

1 teaspoon cinnamon

1 teaspoon nutmeg

½ cup raisins

½ teaspoon lemon juice

4 flour tortillas (see Flour Tortillas, page 286)

What You Do

1. Preheat oven to 350°F.

2. Mash bananas. Peel apple. Remove core and stem. Dice into ¼" pieces.

3. Mix bananas, cinnamon, nutmeg, raisins, apple chunks, and lemon juice together.

4. Place ¼ of the mixture in the middle of each tortilla. Roll up and place on a cookie sheet. Bake for 5 minutes.

How Can I Prevent Fruit From Browning?

To keep fruit such as bananas and apples from turning brown once they have had their peels removed, sprinkle them with a small amount of lemon or lime juice (lime is more commonly used by Mexican cooks). The acid in the juice stops the sugars in the fruits from reacting with the air to produce the brown color.

Banana Fritadas v

What You Need

6 ripe bananas

3 cups flour

½ cup sugar

2 teaspoons cinnamon

1 teaspoon baking powder

2 well-beaten eggs

2 teaspoons vanilla

2 tablespoons vegetable oil

What You Do

1. Peel bananas and mash well.

2. Combine flour, sugar, cinnamon, and baking powder. Mix well. Stir in bananas.

3. Add eggs and vanilla. Stir until ingredients are well blended.

4. In a medium-sized frying pan, heat vegetable oil to medium-high heat. Make hand-sized patties about ½" thick out of the dough. Fry on both sides until light brown.

How Can I Quickly Ripen Fruit?

Almost any fruit will ripen quicker if you put it in a brown paper bag lightly closed in a cool, dry place.

Fruit Compote v

For a special treat, ladle over vanilla ice cream or raspberry sherbet.

What You Need

1½ cups seedless green grapes

1½ cups fresh strawberries

2 medium oranges

4 medium kiwis

2 medium peaches

5 tablespoons confectioners' sugar

3 tablespoons triple sec or Cointreau liqueur

3 tablespoons tequila

1½ tablespoons lime juice

What You Do

1. Wash grapes and cut in half. Wash strawberries, remove stems, and cut in half. Peel oranges and slice into ¼" rounds. Peel kiwis and slice into ¼" rounds. Peel peaches, remove pits, and slice into ¼" thick slices.

2. In a small jar, combine sugar, liqueur, tequila, and lime juice. Cover and shake until well mixed.

3. Combine all fruit in a large serving bowl. Toss to mix. Add dressing and toss fruit until well covered.

4. Cover and refrigerate at least 4 hours before serving.

Mexican Fruitcake v

What You Need

2 eggs

2 cups white sugar

2 cups self-rising flour

2 teaspoons baking soda

1 (20-ounce) can crushed pineapple with juice

1 cup chopped walnuts

1 cup shredded coconut

What You Do

Preheat oven to 350°F. Mix all ingredients thoroughly. Grease and lightly flour a 9" × 13" baking pan. Pour ingredients into pan. Bake for 40 minutes.

Fruit Smoothies v

What You Need

1 banana

⅓ cup fresh mango

⅓ cup fresh papaya

⅓ cup fresh strawberries

⅓ cup fresh peaches

⅔ cup milk

1 teaspoon honey

¼ cup crushed ice

What You Do

Remove skins and seeds from fruit and cut into 1" cubes. Combine all ingredients in blender. Blend on high speed until smooth and frothy.

Can I Substitute Frozen Fruit for Fresh Fruit?

Frozen fruits often don't behave the same as fresh fruits. The act of freezing changes the natural sugars. As a result, many frozen fruits have sugar added. Those that don't often taste bitter. If you must use frozen fruit, especially berries, add extra sugar or honey to the drink.

Surprise your breakfast guests by serving this with Easy Huevos Rancheros (see page 129).

Melon Salad v

What You Need

1 cantaloupe

1 honeydew melon

2–3 jalapeño peppers

1 red bell pepper

1 yellow bell pepper

1 medium Vidalia onion

1 small jicama

4 scallions

1 bunch cilantro

3 tablespoons lime juice

3 tablespoons olive oil

3 tablespoons red cooking sherry

What You Do

1. Remove rind and seeds from cantaloupe and honeydew melons. Cut into 1" cubes. Remove seeds and stems from jalapeño and bell peppers. Cut into ¼" rounds. Peel onion. Cut into ¼" rounds. Peel jicama and cut into ¼" thick strips. Peel scallions and cut into ¼" pieces. Remove stems from cilantro and roughly chop leaves into ½" pieces.

2. Combine melons, peppers, onion, jicama, scallions, and cilantro in a large mixing bowl. Toss until well mixed.

3. In a small jar combine lime juice, olive oil, and cooking sherry. Cover and shake until well blended. Pour over fruit and vegetables. Toss lightly until all covered. Cover and chill in refrigerator for at least 3 hours before serving.

?

How Do I Choose a Ripe Melon?

People say there is an art to finding a ripe melon, but it really is as simple as listening. Lightly thump the melon. It should sound hollow inside. An unripe melon is still dense and will make very little sound when thumped.

Pastelitos v

What You Need

1 cup dried apricots

1 cup water

½ cup sugar

1 teaspoon vanilla extract

2 cups all-purpose flour

¾ teaspoon salt

½ teaspoon baking powder

⅔ cup shortening

5 tablespoons ice water

1 cup confectioners' sugar

3 tablespoons cream

What You Do

1. Preheat oven to 400°F.

2. Put apricots and 1 cup water into a medium saucepan. Cover and bring to a boil. Cook for 20 minutes. Put remaining water and apricots into a blender or food processor and blend until smooth. Combine blended apricots and sugar in saucepan. Cook on medium heat until thick, about 5 minutes. Cool slightly. Stir in ½ teaspoon vanilla extract.

3. Mix flour, salt, and baking powder in a bowl. Cut in shortening until mixture is crumbly. Add ice water, 1 tablespoon at a time. Toss with a fork until dough holds together. Divide dough in half.

4. Roll each half of dough into a 14" × 10" rectangle on a lightly floured surface. Line a 13" × 9" × 2" baking pan with one rectangle of dough. Spread apricot mixture evenly over dough. Place remaining dough on top. Seal edges. Prick the top crust with a fork.

5. Bake for 25 minutes or until lightly browned. Cool slightly.

6. Combine 1 cup confectioners' sugar and ½ teaspoon vanilla extract. Blend in cream. Use as a frosting for the baked pastry. When cool, cut the pastry into squares.

Mango Paste v

What You Need

2 ripe mangos

approximately 4 cups sugar

What You Do

1. Peel the mango and remove the seed.

2. Place the fruit in a food processor or blender and mix on medium setting until you have a purée—the mixture should be free of large lumps.

3. Weigh mango and measure out an equal weight of sugar.

4. Put mango and sugar in a large pot on low heat. Mix well. Cook, stirring often, until the mixture has the consistency of jelly. This usually takes 1–3 hours.

5. Remove from the heat and beat with a large spoon for about 10 minutes or until you have a heavy paste.

6. Pour the paste onto wax paper and set in a sunny area for at least 24 hours.

How Do I Make a Traditional Fruit Paste?

Fruit pastes—or leathers, as Americans call them—are a fun way to recapture pioneer days with children. Instead of keeping the tray in the house, cover it with cheesecloth and let it sit outside for two days in bright sunlight. (Bring it in at night.) That's exactly how people in days gone by processed fruit to store for long trips or long winters.

LEVEL **M**

SERVINGS **6**

This makes an elegant ending to a wonderful meal such as Shrimp in Prickly Pear Vinaigrette (see page 175).

Flaming Fruit v

What You Need

1 fresh mango

3 ripe bananas

1 cup fresh strawberries

1 cup orange juice

2 tablespoons sugar

1 cup tequila

6 large scoops vanilla ice cream

What You Do

1. Wash and peel fresh mango. Cut into 6 slices. Peel bananas and slice lengthwise. Wash strawberries, remove stems, and cut in half.

2. Put fruit in a chafing dish or large skillet on medium heat. Pour orange juice over fruit and sprinkle with sugar. Heat to simmering, stirring gently to dissolve sugar and coat fruit.

3. Put in tequila. Flame sauce by pouring a little tequila into a teaspoon and holding it over a flame until it catches on fire. Put flame in fruit.

4. Serve over ice cream.

What Are Pepitas?

Pepitas are simply the green interior of the pumpkin seed. They are a favorite snack food in Mexico but also a popular cooking ingredient. Note that pumpkin seeds can be eaten with the shell on for a less oily, fruity flavor.

Fruity Tamales v

These are a favorite to take with to the beach. Put the just-steamed tamales in a small cooler to keep them warm.

Tamales are one of the many foods where cornmeal simply cannot be substituted for masa harina without ruining the taste and texture.

What You Need

2 cups masa harina

1 teaspoon salt

1 teaspoon baking powder

⅓ cup shortening

1 cup sugar

1 cup water

1 teaspoon lime juice

60 corn husks

½ cup dried peaches

½ cup dried apricots

½ cup raisins

½ cup slivered almonds

What You Do

1. Mix masa harina, salt, baking powder, shortening, sugar, water, and lime juice in a medium mixing bowl to form a doughy texture. If mixture seems too runny, add more masa, bit by bit. If it seems too dry, add more water, bit by bit.

2. Soak corn husks for 1 hour in warm water. Cut the dried peaches and apricots into ¼" pieces. Mix the peaches, apricots, raisins, and almonds together. Drain husks and pat dry with a paper towel. Overlap 2 cornhusks halfway. Place 1 heaping tablespoon of the masa mixture in the center and spread ¼" thick.

3. Add 1 tablespoon of the fruit mixture to the center of the dough on each corn husk pair. Roll up the husks side to side, so the mixture is centered in the husk, and fold up the ends. Steam for 30 minutes in a steamer lined with an extra dozen corn husks.

?

How Can I Steam without a Steamer?

If you don't have a steamer, add 1" of water to a large pot and place a stainless steel mixing bowl in the pot. Put the tamales in the mixing bowl lined with corn husks and turn the heat on medium-high. Cover and check every 5 minutes to make sure the water doesn't boil away.

Fruity Picadillo

Serve over
white rice and
garnish with fresh
orange slices.

What You Need

3 bananas

3 nectarines

3 pears

1 cup strawberries

2 green apples

1 medium jicama

1 medium yellow onion

3 medium red tomatoes

3 fresh jalapeño peppers

2 tablespoons olive oil

1 pound ground veal

1 pound ground chicken

½ teaspoon cinnamon

½ teaspoon ground cloves

½ cup pistachio meats

What You Do

1. Peel bananas and cut into ½" rounds. Peel nectarines, remove pits, and cut into 1" pieces. Peel pears, remove pits, and cut into 1" pieces. Remove stems from strawberries and slice in half. Peel apples, remove core and stem, and cut into 1" pieces. Peel jicama and cut into 1" pieces. Peel onion and chop into ¼" pieces. Peel tomatoes and chop into ¼" pieces. Remove seeds and stems from jalapeño peppers and cut into ¼" pieces.

2. Heat oil to medium temperature in a large frying pan. Add veal and chicken. Fry on all sides until meat is golden. Add tomatoes, chilies, onion, cinnamon, and cloves. Mix well. Lower heat and cover. Simmer uncovered for 30 minutes, stirring occasionally.

3. Add bananas, nectarines, pears, strawberries, apples, jicama, and pistachios. Stir gently to blend. Cover and simmer for 15 minutes.

Chapter 11

Desserts

Bride's Cookies v

To make these cookies extra special, create a mixture of ½ cup confectioners' sugar and 1 tablespoon cinnamon.

Just when the cookies are cool enough to handle, roll them in the mixture.

What You Need

1 cup unsalted, roasted almonds

2 cups all-purpose flour

½ cup confectioners' sugar

¼ teaspoon salt

1 teaspoon ground cinnamon

1 cup butter, softened

1 teaspoon vanilla extract

What You Do

1. Preheat oven to 350°F.

2. Use a food processor or nut grinder to grind the almonds into small pieces. They should not be a powder.

3. Mix the flour, sugar, salt, cinnamon, and almonds in a medium mixing bowl. Add the softened butter and vanilla. Stir until the ingredients are well blended.

4. Make 24 balls about the size of golf balls and place on cookie sheets.

5. Bake for 20–30 minutes or until lightly browned.

Mexican Chocolate Cake v

Serve this with Coconut Coffee (see page 262), or Mexican Hot Chocolate (see page 302).

What You Need

1¼ cup flour

1 cup granulated sugar

¼ cup cornstarch

5 tablespoons powdered cocoa

1 teaspoon baking soda

1 teaspoon cinnamon

½ teaspoon salt

1 tablespoon white wine vinegar

1 teaspoon vanilla

1 cup cold water

1 tablespoon oil

1 tablespoon corn syrup

2 tablespoons water

1 teaspoon cinnamon

1 cup confectioners' sugar

What You Do

1. Preheat oven to 350°F.

2. Combine flour, granulated sugar, cornstarch, 3 table-spoons powdered cocoa (reserve the other 2 table-spoons for the glaze), baking soda, cinnamon, and salt. Mix well. Add white wine vinegar, vanilla, and cold water. Mix with a fork.

3. Pour mixture into 9" square greased and floured cake pan. Bake 30–35 minutes. Cool cake to room temperature.

4. For glaze, combine 2 tablespoons cocoa, oil, corn syrup, 2 tablespoons water, and cinnamon in a small saucepan. Cook over low heat until ingredi-ents are melded. Add 1 cup confectioners' sugar. Continue cooking, stirring constantly, until sugar is dissolved.

5. Remove glaze from heat and beat until it is smooth and shiny. Spread over the top of the cake. Let cool before serving.

This makes an excellent holiday treat and complements poultry dishes very well.

Almond Custard v

What You Need

2 cups whole milk

6 egg yolks

¼ cup brown sugar

¼ teaspoon salt

1 teaspoon almond extract

½ cup slivered, toasted almonds

What You Do

1. Heat milk in the top of a double boiler until too hot to touch.

2. Separate the eggs and discard the whites. Add the sugar and salt to the egg yolks and beat until light and fluffy.

3. Gradually add egg mixture to milk, stirring constantly. Heat while stirring until the mixture coats a spoon.

4. Remove from heat and cool to room temperature. Add almond extract. Beat until the mixture is firm.

5. Line individual custard dishes with slivered almonds. Pour mixture on top. Place a few almond slivers on the top of each custard. Refrigerate 2 hours before serving.

What Are Plantains?

Most large grocery stores now carry plantains. They are a member of the banana family and look like little bananas. Fresh ones are very dark brown to black on the outside. The inside flesh is significantly heavier than a banana.

Use this as a special treat on a hot summer day.

Serve with Jasmine & Rose Hips Tea (see page 39).

Tropical Gelatin v

What You Need

1 cup papaya

1 cup guava

1 cup fresh pineapple chunks

12 lady fingers

2 cups water

3 (¼-ounce) packages unflavored gelatin

½ cup sugar

What You Do

1. Remove the peels and pits from the papaya and guava and cut into ½" pieces. Measure 1 cup of each fruit and mix together in a small mixing bowl. (Do not drain the juice from the fruit.)

2. Break the lady fingers into 1" pieces and line the bottom of 6 individual custard bowls with the pieces.

3. Bring the 2 cups of water to boil in a medium pot. Add the gelatin and sugar. Stir until both are dissolved. Remove from the heat. Sir in the fruit.

4. Let cool at room temperature until it begins to thicken.

5. Pour mixture over lady fingers. Cool in refrigerator for at least 2 hours before serving.

How Do I Find a Fresh Pineapple?

Fresh, ripe pineapples have a distinctly yellow hue to their rind and smell only mildly sweet while those beyond their freshness will have an almost sickly sweet smell and may even be oozing juice. A green pineapple will be just that—its rind will show very little deep yellow color.

LEVEL **E**

SERVINGS **10**

These treats are as easy as they are tasty.

Even youngsters can make a batch for themselves with little trouble.

Cocoa Pecan Treats v

What You Need

½ cup pecans

½ cup whole milk

2 cups white sugar

½ cup shortening

½ teaspoon salt

½ cup powdered cocoa

3 cups quick-cooking oats

2 teaspoons vanilla

½ cup shredded coconut

What You Do

1. Chop pecans into ⅛" pieces.

2. Put whole milk, sugar, shortening, and salt in saucepan on medium-high heat. Boil for 2 minutes.

3. Remove from heat. Stir in cocoa, oats, vanilla, coconut, and pecans.

4. Drop by rounded teaspoonfuls onto waxed paper. Set in a cool place until treats are room temperature.

?

What Should I Know Before I Bake a Candy Recipe?

Candy is one of the most difficult foods to prepare because you are creating a chemical reaction between the sugars and other ingredients. Always follow the directions exactly and never cook at a higher heat than advised. Scorched milk will ruin a recipe and high heat will create grainy sugar.

LEVEL **E**

SERVINGS **60**

The *fleur-de-lis* shape is traditional for these cookies.

Biscochitos v

What You Need

6 cups flour

3 teaspoons baking powder

1 teaspoon salt

1 pound butter

1¾ cups white sugar

2 teaspoons anise seed

2 eggs

½ cup brandy

1 tablespoon ground cinnamon

What You Do

1. Preheat oven to 350°F.

2. Sift flour with baking powder and salt.

3. Cream butter with 1½ cup sugar and anise seed using a mixer on medium speed.

4. Beat eggs until light and fluffy and add to the creamed mixture. Add flour mixture and brandy. Mix until well blended. Dough should be stiff. If not, add more flour bit by bit until it is.

5. Knead dough and roll out until ¼" to ½" thick. Cut with cookie cutters.

6. Mix remaining ¼ cup sugar and 1 tablespoon ground cinnamon. Use to dust the top of each cookie.

7. Place on cookie sheet and bake 10–12 minutes or until lightly browned.

Traditionally, these cookies are made into 3" circles, although you can cut them into any shape you would like.

Wine Cookies v

What You Need

1 cup margarine

1 cup white sugar

1 egg

1 teaspoon salt

4 cups flour

¼ cup sweet sherry

What You Do

1. Preheat oven to 350°F.

2. Mix margarine and sugar until creamy. Add egg and beat until mixture is light and fluffy.

3. Blend in salt and 2 cups flour. Stir in ¼ cup sweet sherry. Add remaining 2 cups flour and mix well.

4. Chill for 1 hour in refrigerator or until firm.

5. Roll dough on a lightly floured surface until it's about ⅛" thick. Cut with cookie cutters.

6. Place on a lightly greased cookie sheet and bake for 10 minutes.

LEVEL **E**

SERVINGS **4**

Serve as a light dessert after Mexican Pot Roast (see page 103).

Orange Liqueur Mousse v

What You Need

1 (3-ounce) package orange flavored gelatin

1 cup boiling water

¼ cup cold water

¼ cup orange liqueur

1 cup whipping cream

½ teaspoon cinnamon

½ cup shredded coconut

What You Do

1. Dissolve gelatin in boiling water. Add cold water and cool mixture to room temperature. Stir in orange liqueur. Chill in refrigerator until mixture starts to thicken, about 30 minutes.

2. Whip cream until it piles softly. Gradually add gelatin mixture and cinnamon, stirring gently until evenly blended. Pour into mold. Chill until set.

3. Turn mold onto serving plate and top with shredded coconut.

How Can I Make a Recipe Nonalcoholic?

If you want to make uncooked foods calling for liquor nonalcoholic, simply substitute 1 tablespoon of the flavored extract mixed with half water and half corn syrup. You will get a very similar flavor without the alcohol.

Pepita Balls v

What You Need

1 pound unsalted pepitas

1 cup sweetened condensed milk

3½ cups confectioners' sugar

What You Do

1. Grind pepitas finely.

2. Mix pepitas with sweetened condensed milk and 3 cups confectioners' sugar.

3. Shape into 1" balls and roll in remaining confectioners' sugar. Place on wax paper on a cookie sheet.

4. Refrigerate 2–3 hours or until set.

Key Lime Pie v

What You Need

1 refrigerated or frozen (thawed) pie crust

3 eggs

1 (14-ounce) can sweetened condensed milk

½ cup fresh squeezed Key lime juice

3 teaspoons grated Key lime peel

¾ cups whipping cream

2 tablespoons confectioners' sugar

What You Do

1. Preheat oven to 350°F. Place pie crust in oven for 10 minutes.

2. Beat eggs, milk, lime juice, and 2 teaspoons grated lime peel on medium speed in a medium-sized mixing bowl. Pour into pie crust.

3. Bake 30–35 minutes or until center is set. Cool on wire rack for 15 minutes. Cover and refrigerate 2–8 hours.

4. No more than 4 hours before serving, put whipping cream, 1 teaspoon grated lime peel, and confectioners' sugar into a well-chilled bowl and whip until it doubles in size. Spread on top of pie.

LEVEL Ⓔ

SERVINGS ⑥

Serve as dessert
after Shrimp
in Prickly Pear
Vinaigrette (see
page 175).

Mexican Trifle ᵥ

What You Need

¼ cup sugar

1 tablespoon cornstarch

¼ teaspoon salt

2 cups whole milk

2 eggs

1 teaspoon vanilla

4 cups cubed pound cake

4 tablespoons brandy

4 tablespoons apricot preserves

½ cup whipped cream

1 tablespoon confectioners' sugar

4 ounces semi-sweet baker's chocolate

½ cup toasted, slivered almonds

What You Do

1. Combine sugar, cornstarch, and salt in a saucepan. Stir in milk until well blended. Cook over medium heat, stirring constantly, until mixture boils.

2. Break eggs into a medium mixing bowl. Add about ¼ cup of sugar mixture to eggs and beat slightly. Add the egg mixture to the sugar mixture and cook on medium heat, stirring constantly until mixture starts to bubble. Stir in vanilla. Remove from heat, cover with waxed paper, and let cool to room temperature.

3. Place cubes of pound cake in a glass bowl. Sprinkle with 3 tablespoons brandy. Drizzle with preserves. Pour sugar and egg mixture (which should be like a custard when cooled) over the pound cake.

4. Whip cream with confectioners' sugar until stiff. Fold in 1 tablespoon brandy. Top cake and custard with whipped cream.

5. Grate chocolate. Sprinkle chocolate and almonds on top of cake.

6. Cover and chill at least 4 hours before serving.

Although it's traditionally served over ice, this tea also is excellent served warm with Bride's Cookies (see page 250).

Pumpkin Seed Tea v

What You Need

2 cups pumpkin seeds

1 Key lime

8 cups water

½ cup honey

What You Do

1. Put the pumpkin seeds in a food processor or blender and grind until you have a coarse powder.

2. Cut the lime into ¼" rounds.

3. Put the water, lime, and pumpkin seeds in a covered glass jar and store in a warm place for 6–12 hours.

4. Strain the water and discard the pumpkin seed mash as well as the lime pieces. Stir in ½ cup honey.

LEVEL **E**

SERVINGS **8**

Serve this coffee with Capirotada (see page 299).

Coconut Coffee v

What You Need

16 tablespoons ground coffee

½ cup coconut milk

¼ cup shredded coconut

8 cups water

What You Do

1. Using a percolator or drip coffee maker, place shredded coconut and ground coffee together in the filter of the coffee maker.

2. Fill the coffee maker with 8 cups of water and brew as you normally would.

3. Stir in the half cup of coconut milk before serving. Top with a few strands of grated coconut.

?

What's Better: Perked or Dripped Coffee?

Most North Americans have adopted the drip coffee maker for its convenience but there is a lot to be said for the old-fashioned percolator. A drip coffee maker filters out all of the flavorful oils that give coffee its robust flavor. If you're looking for a special treat for your dessert coffee, trying digging out the percolator. You'll notice the difference.

This bread is frequently served at holiday celebrations.

Rosquillas Fritas v

What You Need

4 cups vegetable oil

2 teaspoons active dry yeast

¼ cup warm water

½ cup roasted almonds

3 cups flour

2 eggs

1¼ cup white sugar

1 teaspoon baking soda

½ teaspoon salt

½ teaspoon almond extract or flavoring

½ teaspoon cinnamon

2 tablespoons butter

¼ cup whole milk

½ cup confectioners' sugar (or ½ cup white sugar with or without 1 tablespoon cinnamon)

What You Do

1. Pour vegetable oil into a medium skillet. Oil should be about 2" deep. Heat to about 370°F. Dissolve yeast in ¼ cup warm water. Chop almonds into small pieces.

2. Mix half of the flour with eggs, white sugar, dissolved yeast, baking soda, salt, almond extract, almonds, cinnamon, butter, and whole milk. Beat until the dough begins to thicken. Add the remaining flour and mix well. If the dough is not stiff enough to knead, sprinkle more flour, a handful at a time.

3. Spread flour over a flat surface and remove the dough from the bowl. Knead the dough until it is pliable and smooth. Roll the dough about ½" thick and cut into doughnut shapes.

4. Put 2 to 3 fritas in the hot oil at a time. Fry for 2–3 minutes or until golden brown. Flip and fry 2–3 minutes on the other side. Place on paper towels to dry. Sprinkle with confectioners' sugar, white sugar, or a mixture of sugar and cinnamon.

Torrejas de Coco v

While many people call this Mexican-style French toast, it actually is used as a dessert in Mexico.

What You Need

1½ pound loaf of cooked egg bread

¼ cup blanched almonds

4 cups sugar

1½ cup water

2 cups shredded coconut

3 eggs

1 tablespoon flour

1 cup shortening

1 cinnamon stick

3 tablespoons raisins

What You Do

1. Slice egg bread into 24 slices. Chop almonds into small pieces.

2. Dissolve 1 cup sugar in ½ cup water in a saucepan over medium heat. Bring to a boil and boil for 3 minutes. Add shredded coconut. Cook about 15 minutes. Remove from heat and cool slightly.

3. Spread coconut paste on 12 slices of egg bread, then cover each with another slice.

4. Beat eggs with flour. Dip both sides of sandwiches in egg.

5. Heat shortening in a large frying pan to medium-high heat. Fry sandwiches on each side about 1 minute. Set on paper towels to cool.

6. Make a syrup by heating 3 cups sugar, cinnamon stick, and 1 cup water to boiling in a large frying pan. Boil 5 minutes. Add browned sandwiches, reduce heat and simmer for 5 minutes. Turn the sandwiches over and simmer an additional 5 minutes.

7. Arrange sandwiches on a serving dish. Garnish with raisins and almonds. Top with strained syrup.

For a different version, replace the coffee with a cup of whole milk and add a ½ cup of ground pistachios to the mixture instead of the coffee and cinnamon.

Coffee Caramel   v

What You Need

7 cups whole milk

3 cups sugar

1 teaspoon baking soda

1 cup hot, strong coffee

½ teaspoon cinnamon

2 tablespoons butter

What You Do

1. Combine milk, sugar, and baking soda in a large pot on medium heat.

2. Boil, stirring every few minutes, until the mixture turns thick and slightly brown.

3. Add the hot, strong coffee and cinnamon. Stir well.

4. Turn heat to low and continue cooking until the mixture is thick. When a small drop of the mixture is put in a glass of cold water, it should form a soft ball.

5. Spread the butter onto the bottom and sides of a 9" × 9" cake pan. Pour the mixture into the pan. Chill in the refrigerator at least 2 hours before serving.

Mexican Tea Cakes v

Although enjoyed the year-round, these are a traditional Christmas holiday treat.

What You Need

¼ cup pistachio meats

1 cup butter

2½ cups flour

1¾ cup confectioners' sugar

2 teaspoons vanilla

½ teaspoon salt

1 teaspoon cinnamon

What You Do

1. Grind pistachio meats. Soften butter in a medium mixing bowl by stirring with a spoon.

2. Add flour, pistachio meats, ¾ cup confectioners' sugar, vanilla, and salt. Mix to make a stiff dough.

3. Cover and chill in refrigerator for 2–4 hours.

4. Preheat oven to 350°F.

5. Form dough into balls about 1" in diameter. Place on greased cookie sheet in oven for 10–15 minutes. Cookies should be firm but not brown.

6. Remove and roll in 1 cup confectioners' sugar mixed with 1 teaspoon cinnamon. When cool, roll cakes in sugar and cinnamon mixture again.

? What's Mexican Chocolate?

Mexican chocolate desserts often taste less sweet and chocolatey than those we're used to in the United States. If you want a less traditional taste but one you're more familiar with, double the chocolate and sugar, and don't add the vinegar in the dessert recipes calling for chocolate.

LEVEL **M**

SERVINGS **8**

This light custard is perfect after a spicy, heavy meal of chicken or beef.

Natillas v

What You Need

4 eggs

½ cup flour

1 quart milk

¾ cup sugar

⅛ teaspoon salt

1 teaspoon nutmeg

1 teaspoon cinnamon

What You Do

1. Separate eggs and make a paste of the egg yolks, flour, and 1 cup milk.

2. In a medium saucepan, add the sugar and salt to the remaining milk and scald at medium heat. Add the egg yolk mixture to the scalded milk and continue to cook at medium temperature until it reaches the consistency of soft custard. Remove from heat and cool to room temperature.

3. Beat the egg whites until stiff. Fold into the custard.

4. Cover and chill at least 2 hours before serving.

5. Spoon into individual dishes and sprinkle with nutmeg and cinnamon right before serving.

?

Are Custards and Puddings Popular in Mexico?

Mexicans enjoy custards and puddings in their diet, perhaps because they are an excellent way to get more milk into the diet. They also are a fun way to use the many spices available in this culture.

Pistachio Coconut Flan   v

What You Need

6 large eggs

1 (14-ounce) can sweetened condensed milk

2 teaspoons vanilla extract

2 cups whole milk

2 cups half and half

2 tablespoons grated coconut

1 tablespoon ground pistachio meats

What You Do

1. Preheat the oven to 325°F.

2. In a large mixing bowl, gently stir together the eggs, sweetened condensed milk, and vanilla extract.

3. Pour the milk and half and half into a medium saucepan and place on the stove on medium-high heat. Bring the milk and half and half to a boil, then remove from heat. Gradually pour the egg mixture into the hot milk, stirring constantly to make sure the eggs don't clump.

4. Pour the mixture through a strainer into a greased, 9" cake pan. Sprinkle coconut and pistachio meats on top. Place the pan into a large roasting pan and fill the roasting pan with warm tap water until it is about halfway up the sides of the cake pan.

5. Bake for 60 minutes. The center should feel firm when pressed, but not be browned. The edges may be slightly browned. Remove from oven and set aside until room temperature. Cover and refrigerate for at least 4 hours before serving.

Pistachios and almonds can be substituted for the pecans to complement different dishes.

Pecan Pudding v

What You Need

½ cup roasted pecans

1 cup water

1 (¼-ounce) envelope unflavored gelatin

½ teaspoon vanilla extract

1 cup white sugar

6 egg whites

What You Do

1. Use a food processor or nut grinder to break the pecans into small pieces. However, they should not make a powder.

2. Put water in a medium pot on high heat. When boiling, add the gelatin. Stir until the gelatin is dissolved.

3. Add the vanilla extract and sugar and stir until it is dissolved.

4. Cool until the mixture begins to thicken.

5. Beat the whites until they form stiff peaks. Fold the egg whites into the gelatin mixture until well blended. Gently stir in the pecans.

6. Pour into individual cups and chill until firm.

?

What's the Difference Between Extracts and Flavorings?

Extracts are flavorings that have actually been extracted from the fruit or seed by squashing it and removing the oil. Flavorings are usually artificially produced and added to a water base.

Many cultures have a rice pudding, but this one is the ultimate.

Its subtle flavors instantly transport you to a coastal resort.

Raisin & Pistachio Pudding   v

What You Need

½ cup roasted pistachio meats

½ cup raisins

1 cup dry white wine

1 Key lime

1 cup water

½ cup uncooked rice

¼ teaspoon salt

4 cups whole milk

1 cup sugar

1 teaspoon cinnamon

2 egg yolks

What You Do

1. Grind the pistachios in a nut grinder or food processor until you have small pieces. They should not be powder. Put the raisins and white wine in a small mixing bowl and set aside. Remove the rind from the Key lime and discard the fruit.

2. Bring 1 cup water to a boil in a medium-sized pan. Add the rice, salt, and lime rind. Cover and boil for 5 minutes then reduce heat to low and simmer for 15 minutes.

3. Discard the lime rind. Add the milk, sugar, and cinnamon. Continue cooking uncovered on low heat, stirring occasionally, until all the milk has been absorbed.

4. Beat the egg yolks. Discard the wine that has not soaked into the raisins. Mix the egg yolks, raisins, and pistachios into the rice mixture. Cook 5 minutes.

5. Place pudding in a serving dish, cover, and refrigerate at least 2 hours before serving.

Mexican Carrot Cake v

Serve with Mexican
Coffee (see page
303), or Mexican
Hot Chocolate (see
page 302).

What You Need

8 medium carrots

4 teaspoons lemon rind

4 teaspoons lemon juice

1 teaspoon vanilla extract

6 tablespoons sugar

¼ cup vegetable oil

4 medium eggs

4 flour tortillas (see Flour Tortillas, page 286)

What You Do

1. Preheat oven to 350°F.

2. Peel carrots then grate finely. Grate lemon rind.

3. In a small bowl, combine carrots, lemon rind, lemon juice, and vanilla extract. Set aside.

4. Combine sugar with vegetable oil. Stir in eggs. Tear or cut tortillas into ¼" pieces. Add tortillas and carrot mixture to sugar and egg mixture. Mix well.

5. Bake in a 9" Springform pan for 1 hour or until top is brown.

What Kind of Carrots Should I Use in a Dessert Dish?

When using carrots in a dessert dish, be sure to use medium or small carrots. They contain the most flavor and the most juice. Large carrots are fine with meat or vegetable dishes but they are too acidic and flat-tasting for desserts.

If you're used to pralines from America's Southeast, these will taste a little odd at first. However, this authentic candy complements a Mexican meal perfectly.

Pecan Candy v

What You Need

2 cups white sugar

½ cup margarine

1 cup canned condensed milk

2 tablespoons white corn syrup

1 teaspoon vanilla extract

¼ teaspoon cayenne pepper

½ teaspoon chili powder

3 cups pecans

What You Do

1. Combine sugar, margarine, condensed milk, and corn syrup in a medium pot. Heat on medium-high until mixture forms a firm, soft ball when a small amount is dropped into cold water.

2. Remove from heat. Stir in vanilla, cayenne pepper, chili powder, and pecans.

3. Using a tablespoon, drop into patties on waxed paper. Put in a cool place until room temperature.

?

Are Each Side of a Piece of Waxed Paper the Same?

Waxed paper actually has only one side that is waxed. If you put the food on the wrong side it is likely to stick, although the paper used is fairly slick so it won't stick as much as if you had put it on newspaper or typing paper. You can find the right side by running your fingernail over the paper. Your fingernail will collect a tiny amount of wax if you're on the right side.

This makes a perfect ending to a romantic meal such as Shrimp in Prickly Pear Vinaigrette (see page 175).

Wine Custard v

What You Need

6 cups whole milk

2 cups sugar

¼ cup heavy red wine

What You Do

1. Place milk in the top of a double boiler and heat over boiling water. Stir in sugar. Cook for 2 hours, stirring occasionally. Remove from heat and let cool to room temperature.

2. Pour milk mixture into a saucepan on medium-low heat. Stir in wine until the wine is completely absorbed. Put in a serving dish. Cover and chill 3–4 hours before serving.

Pineapple & Almond Pudding ᵥ

This is a perfect dessert to complement the rich flavors in Chicken Tablecloth Stainer (see page 149).

What You Need

4 egg yolks

½ cup blanched almonds

1 angel food cake

2 cups fresh or canned pineapple chunks, drained

½ cup plus 1 tablespoon sugar

½ cup dry sherry

¼ teaspoon ground cinnamon

½ cup orange marmalade

½ cup sour cream

½ cup toasted, slivered almonds

What You Do

1. Beat egg yolks. Grind blanched almonds. Cut angel food cake into twelve 4" × 1" slices.

2. Combine pineapple, ½ cup sugar, ¼ cup sherry, egg yolks, and cinnamon in a medium saucepan. Cook over low heat, stirring constantly, until thickened. Remove from heat to cool.

3. Spread cake slices with marmalade. Arrange half the cake slices in the bottom of a 1½ quart serving dish. Sprinkle with 2 tablespoons sherry. Spoon half the pineapple mixture on top. Repeat layers of cake slices, sherry, and pineapple mixture. Cover and refrigerate 2–3 hours.

4. Mix remaining 1 tablespoon sugar into sour cream. Spread over the top of the chilled dessert. Decorate with toasted slivered almonds.

❓ What's the Secret to Good Rice?

You can't peek at rice once you set it to simmer. Even waterlogged rice is salvageable by baking it in the oven for 30 minutes at 300°F. But, if you peek at it when you shouldn't, you will lose the value of the steaming process and could end up with a sticky, gooey mess.

This is traditionally served as a dessert but makes an excellent vegetable course when served with a beef or pork dish.

Sugared Pumpkin v

What You Need

1 medium pumpkin

½ cup butter

2 tablespoons cinnamon

2 cups brown sugar

What You Do

1. Preheat oven to 350°F.

2. Cut pumpkin into pieces approximately 6" square, removing the seeds, interior fibers, and outer peel.

3. Poke holes in the pumpkin flesh with a fork. Spread a thin layer of butter on each pumpkin piece.

4. Mix the cinnamon and brown sugar together and spread on the pumpkin pieces.

5. Place in a baking dish and bake for 1–2 hours or until a fork slides easily into the flesh.

This is the perfect dessert for a traditional Mexican meal such as Beef Tamales (see page 309).

Pecan Cake   v

What You Need

3 eggs

½ cup pecans

½ cup butter

¾ cup cake flour

1 teaspoon baking powder

⅔ cup sugar

1 tablespoon lemon juice

½ teaspoon salt

½ cup orange marmalade

¼ cup sugar

What You Do

1. Preheat oven to 350°F.

2. Separate eggs. Finely grate pecans. Melt butter in a small saucepan on low heat. Blend flour and baking powder.

3. Beat egg yolks in a mixing bowl until they are thick and lemon-colored. Gradually beat in ⅔ cup sugar. Beat in lemon juice and grated pecans. Gradually beat in flour mixture. Slowly beat in melted butter.

4. Beat egg whites with salt until stiff peaks form. Fold beaten egg whites into batter. Pour batter into a greased and floured 9" round cake pan. Bake 30–35 minutes or until a toothpick inserted in the center comes out clean. Let cake cool 10 minutes before removing from pan.

5. Combine ½ cup orange marmalade and ¼ cup sugar in a small saucepan. Cook until sugar is dissolved, stirring constantly. While still warm, use as a glaze for the cake.

?

What's Self-Rising Flour?

Self-rising flour is simply flour that contains baking powder. When water is added and the dish is placed in the oven, the baking powder activates and begins to rise. If you don't have self-rising flour, add 1½ tablespoons of baking powder for every 2 cups of flour.

These traditional Christmas treats are a favorite with young children.

Christmas Candy Balls   v

What You Need

2 medium white potatoes

2 cups pecans

1 cup red candied cherries

1 cup confectioners' sugar

1 teaspoon ground cinnamon

1 cup sugar

1 teaspoon vanilla extract

What You Do

1. Scrub potatoes but do not peel. Cut into 1" cubes. Chop pecans into small pieces. Cut candied cherries in half. Mix confectioners' sugar and cinnamon in a small bowl.

2. Put potatoes in a medium-sized pot. Add water to cover. Bring to a boil and continue boiling until potatoes are soft. Drain water.

3. Press potatoes through a ricer or put through a food mill. Mix in sugar, vanilla extract, and nuts.

4. Form balls about the size of marbles. Coat them with confectioners' sugar and cinnamon mixture.

5. Store in refrigerator until ready to serve. Put into small fluted paper cups and garnish with cherry halves.

What's Ginger Root?

Ginger can come in many forms, from jellied and crystallized to ground and pickled. Fresh ginger root should have a silvery skin. It will have a slightly spicy flavor. To prepare it, first remove the tough outer skin with a heavy blade. It then can be chopped or grated.

These can be made
using any jam or
heated fruits.

Pineapple Sopaillas v

What You Need

2 cups flour

1 tablespoon baking powder

1 teaspoon salt

4 ¼ cups peanut oil

¾ cup water

3 cups canned chunk pineapple, drained

2 tablespoons cinnamon

1 cup white sugar

What You Do

1. Mix flour, baking powder, and salt in a medium mixing bowl.

2. Blend ¼ cup oil into dry ingredients. Stir in just enough water to make a soft dough.

3. Divide dough into 4 parts. Roll 1 part at a time to about ¼" thick. Cut into triangles about 4" × 2".

4. In a large skillet, heat the remaining peanut oil to about 385°F. Add 3 to 4 pieces of dough at a time. Stir the oil until pieces puff like pillows. Fry until light brown. Lay on paper towels to drain grease.

5. Heat pineapple to lukewarm in a small saucepan over medium-low heat.

6. Open a small hole in the side of each puff and spoon about 2 tablespoons of pineapple into each.

7. Mix cinnamon and sugar. Use to sprinkle the top of each puff.

Vary the types of nuts used and add a mixture of lemon and orange rinds for a completely different treat.

Mexican Orange v

What You Need

2 orange rinds

1 cup pistachio nuts

1½ cups condensed milk

3 cups white sugar

½ cup butter

What You Do

1. Cut orange rind into ¼" pieces. Chop nuts into small pieces.

2. Place condensed milk into the top of a double boiler and heat until scalded—milk will have a film on top.

3. Melt 1 cup sugar in a large kettle on medium-high heat until it is a rich yellow color. Add hot milk to the sugar. Add 2 cups sugar, stir, and cook until it reaches 238°F on a candy thermometer.

4. Remove from heat. Stir in rind, butter, and nuts.

5. Pour into a buttered 7" × 11" pan and place in a cool area until room temperature.

This is frequently used as a birthday or anniversary cake.

Cream-Filled Chestnut Cake

What You Need

6 eggs

1¾ pound fresh chestnuts in the shell

¾ cup butter

1 cup sugar

1 teaspoon vanilla extract

1¼ cups flour

1 teaspoon baking powder

½ cup whole milk

1 cup whipping cream

⅔ cup confectioners' sugar

What You Do

1. Preheat oven to 350°F. Separate eggs.

2. To prepare chestnuts, rinse chestnuts and make a slit on two sides of each shell. Put into a saucepan. Cover with boiling water and boil about 20 minutes. Remove shells and skins. Return chestnuts to saucepan and cover with boiling salted water. Cover and simmer until chestnuts are tender (10 to 20 minutes). Drain and finely chop.

3. Cream butter with sugar and ½ teaspoon vanilla extract until fluffy. Add 1¼ cups of the chopped chestnuts then the egg yolks one at a time. Mix well after each egg yolk is added.

4. Mix flour with baking powder and add to the chestnut mixture. Mix well and add milk. Mix well.

5. Beat egg whites until stiff but not dry. Fold into batter.

Cream-Filled Chestnut Cake—continued

6. Divide mixture among two greased and floured 9" round cake pans. Bake 25 minutes.

7. Whip 1 cup whipping cream until thickened. Mix in confectioners' sugar and ½ teaspoon vanilla extract. Blend in remaining chopped chestnuts. Place a generous portion on the top of the bottom layer of the cake. Add top layer and use remaining mixture to frost entire cake.

Molasses Candy   v

What You Need

1 cup light molasses

1 cup firmly packed brown sugar

2 tablespoons butter

1 teaspoon cider vinegar

¼ teaspoon almond extract

1½ cups toasted, slivered almonds

What You Do

1. Put molasses, brown sugar, butter, and vinegar into a heavy saucepan. Bring to a boil. Boil hard 7–12 minutes or until mixture reaches 260°F on a candy thermometer. Mixture should form a firm ball when a small amount is dropped in cold water.

2. Remove from heat. Add almond extract and almonds. Stir well. Pour onto a greased baking sheet. Spread as thin as possible. Let cool.

3. Break into 2" pieces.

Chapter 12
Traditional Favorites

Chili Powder v

*This recipe yields
⅔ cup.

This is a recipe that
requires adjusting
to fit your individual
taste. Remember,
chili powder is
about taste and
seasoning, not
just making food
taste hot.

What You Need

1–1½ cups dried chilies

1 tablespoon ground cumin

2 teaspoons paprika

½ teaspoon garlic powder

What You Do

1. Cut off stems of dried chilies. Grind all ingredients together into a fine powder in a blender, food processor, or coffee/spice grinder.

2. Store in an airtight container. Glass works best.

3. Vary the flavor of this by using different dried chilies in different proportions. A combination gives the best flavor—put at least one tiny hot one in.

Where Can I Purchase Ethnic Spices?

If your local grocery store doesn't carry certain ethnic spices or ingredients, you may be able to find them on the Internet or at specialty shops. Just make sure to stock up on shelf-stable necessities so you can make these dishes whenever you like.

Basic Corn Tortillas v

As a basic ingredient in Mexican cooking, you may want to make large batches of these ahead of time and freeze them.

To know when the cooking surface is the right temperature, fling a drop of cold water onto it.

When it sizzles, you're ready to cook.

What You Need

2 cups masa harina (do not substitute cornmeal)

½ teaspoon salt

1¼ cup warm water (plus a little more if needed)

What You Do

1. Mix masa harina and salt and add water a little at a time. Mix into a soft dough. The dough should not stick to your hands, but it should be moist. If it is too dry, add water a little at a time. If sticky, add masa harina, 1 teaspoon (or less) at a time until it doesn't stick any longer.

2. Divide the dough and roll into balls about the size of golf balls.

3. Flatten the balls between two sheets of wax paper. Flatten quite thin with a rolling pin, small plate, or tortilla press to a 6" diameter.

4. Place each tortilla separately in a preheated ungreased frying pan, griddle, or cast-iron *placa* and cook over medium heat until slightly brown, usually 1 to 2 minutes. Flip and cook on the other side until slightly brown at the edges. Tortillas should still be soft and flexible.

(?)

What are *Placas* and *Comals*?

When making or warming tortillas, Mexican cooks use a cast-iron placa (imagine a cast-iron skillet without sides or an old woodstove lid) or a comal (an earthenware version). Though comals are rare outside of the Southwest, placas are showing up all over the United States. If you can't find one and have a Scandinavian store near, look for what the Swedes call a *plat*. It's the same thing.

Flour Tortillas v

For a different taste, grind up jalapeño peppers and add to the dough or use whole wheat flour.

Tortillas should only be cooked once on each side.

What You Need

2 cups flour

½ teaspoon salt

1 teaspoon baking soda

¼ cup lard or shortening

½ cup cold water (plus extra if needed)

What You Do

1. Mix flour, salt, and baking soda. Using a pastry cutter or two forks, cut the lard or shortening into the dry ingredients until the mixture forms crumbles the size of small peas. Add water bit by bit and mix into a smooth, elastic dough. If dough sticks to your hand, sprinkle more flour on the dough a little at a time until it doesn't stick.

2. Divide the dough and roll into balls about the size of golf balls. Cover the dough while cooking tortillas.

3. Flatten the balls between two sheets of wax paper, using your hands and a rolling pin until 10–12" in diameter.

4. Cook tortillas on a preheated, ungreased griddle or placa until they bubble up. Flip and cook on the other side, or until lightly browned.

LEVEL **E**

SERVINGS *

*This recipe yield depends on the number of tortillas used.

For tortilla chips, simply break the tostadas into the desired size pieces.

For a unique taste, sprinkle with dry ranch dressing mix.

Tostadas v

What You Need

½ cup vegetable oil

Corn tortillas (see Basic Corn Tortillas, page 285)

½ teaspoon salt

What You Do

1. Spread oil evenly over bottom of a large frying pan. Preheat to medium-high temperature.

2. Place tortillas in hot oil one at a time and fry until crisp. Flip the tortillas when one side is brown to ensure even cooking.

3. Sprinkle with salt while cooking.

4. Place on paper towels to drain.

LEVEL **E**

SERVINGS **10**

If you would rather use fresh-made dough for the sweet rolls, look at the dough recipe for Pineapple Sopaillas (see page 278).

Easy Mexican Sweet Rolls v

What You Need

¼ cup butter

2 eggs

⅔ cup flour

½ cup white sugar

1 (10-ounce) can refrigerator flaky biscuits

½ teaspoon shortening

1 tablespoon whole milk

What You Do

1. Preheat oven to 375°F.

2. Soften butter by placing in a warm place. Separate eggs. Combine flour and sugar in a bowl. Cut in butter until mixture resembles coarse crumbs. Add egg yolks. Mix until well blended. Set aside ¼ cup of this mixture.

3. Separate canned biscuits into 10 pieces. Press or roll each to a ⅗ thick oval. Crumble 1–2 tablespoons of sugar and flour mixture over each oval to ¼" of edge.

4. Roll biscuit, starting at shorter side, wrapping dough around filling and rolling to opposite side. Place seam-side down on cookie sheet lightly greased with shortening.

5. Beat egg whites with milk. Brush over rolls with a pastry brush. Sprinkle evenly with reserved ¼ cup of sugar and flour mixture. Press lightly into rolls. Bake for 13–17 minutes or until medium brown.

What's an Easy Way to Separate Eggs?

If you don't have an egg separator in your kitchen, break the egg neatly in half and transfer the yolk back and forth from shell to shell, catching the white in a small bowl underneath. In some recipes even the smallest amount of yolk in an egg white can cause the recipe to fail, so don't break that yolk!

Mexican Spoon Bread

This is used as a side dish to meals that don't have tortillas.

Spoon it out as you would mashed potatoes.

What You Need

½ cup shortening

1 cup cornmeal

2 eggs

1 can cream-style corn

1 teaspoon salt

½ cup milk

½ teaspoon baking soda

¼ cup canned sliced jalapeño peppers

1 pound shredded Cheddar cheese

What You Do

1. Preheat oven to 350°F.

2. Melt shortening in a small saucepan on medium heat.

3. Mix cornmeal and eggs together until well blended. Add the corn, shortening, salt, milk, and baking soda. Mix well.

4. Pour half of the mixture into a greased 9" × 9" casserole. Add a layer of jalapeño peppers and half the cheese. Add the remaining mixture and top with the rest of the cheese.

5. Place in oven and bake for 45–50 minutes or until lightly browned.

Gazpacho makes an excellent first course to a heavier beef or chicken meal.

It also makes a good lunch served with bread and cheese.

Gazpacho v

What You Need

4 large tomatoes

1 small yellow onion

1 green bell pepper

2 medium carrots

2 stalks celery

4 cups canned tomato soup

2 tablespoons olive oil

2 tablespoons wine vinegar

2 teaspoons salt

1 teaspoon ground black pepper

1 medium cucumber

What You Do

1. Peel tomatoes and cut into quarters. Remove skin from onion and cut in quarters. Remove stem and seeds from green bell pepper and cut in quarters. Peel carrots and cut in quarters. Remove leaves from celery and cut in quarters.

2. Combine 2 cups tomato soup, olive oil, wine vinegar, salt, pepper, and half of tomatoes, onion, peppers, carrots, and celery in a blender. Blend until liquid, about 1 minute. Pour in a bowl.

3. Repeat with remaining tomato soup and vegetables. Combine with previous mixture.

4. Cover and chill in refrigerator for at least 2 hours before serving.

5. Cut cucumber into thin slices and place on top right before serving.

Garnish with grated
Cheddar cheese
and sour cream.

Black Bean Soup v

What You Need

2 cups dried black beans

2½ quarts water

½ cup vegetable oil

1 cup chopped onions

½ teaspoon garlic paste

½ teaspoon ground black pepper

¼ teaspoon fennel

¼ teaspoon basil

1 teaspoon sugar

1 teaspoon dried mustard

1 teaspoon grated lemon rind

¼ teaspoon allspice

1 teaspoon dried cilantro

1 cup canned tomato sauce

½ teaspoon salt

3 tablespoons lemon juice

What You Do

1. Soak beans overnight in ½ quart water or use Quick & Easy Beans (see page 210) process to prepare for cooking.

2. Combine all ingredients except lemon juice and salt in a large soup pot. Stir until well blended. Bring to a boil then lower temperature to medium-low. Simmer uncovered for 2 hours or until beans are soft.

3. Add salt and lemon juice and stir right before serving.

Where Can I Shop for Beans?

Although we think of only a couple types of beans, there are many, many varieties that Mexicans routinely use. Traditional grocery stores are beginning to carry more of these varieties, but you also might try a local food co-op. Virtually any bean can be substituted in these recipes, depending on your taste.

Chicken Chalupas

Serve with Spinach Salad (see page 89) and Fruit Compote (see page 241).

What You Need

12 corn tortillas (see Basic Corn Tortillas, page 285)

1¼ cup chicken stock (see Chicken Stock, page 124)

1 cup sour cream

2 cups Spicy Chicken (see page 125)

1 pound shredded Monterey jack cheese

1 teaspoon paprika

What You Do

1. Soak tortillas in 1 cup of the chicken stock. Combine remaining ¼ cup chicken stock with sour cream.

2. Layer ingredients in a casserole as follows: single layer of soaked tortillas, Spicy Chicken, chicken sauce, cheese. Repeat until all ingredients are used. Sprinkle with paprika.

3. Cover and refrigerate at least 8 hours.

4. Preheat oven to 350°F. When oven is heated, bake dish uncovered for 1 hour.

Serve with Zesty
Cheese Salad (see
page 92).

Traditional Pollo Verde

What You Need

1 medium white onion

1 garlic clove

2 fresh tomatillos

1 cup Green Chili Sauce (see page 18)

1 bunch fresh parsley

1 teaspoon salt

1 teaspoon ground white pepper

1 frying chicken, cut-up

What You Do

1. Peel onion and cut into quarters. Peel garlic. Remove stems and peels from tomatillos then cut in half.

2. Put onion, garlic, Green Chili Sauce, tomatillos, parsley, salt, and white pepper in a blender or food processor. Blend until liquefied.

3. Rinse chicken and arrange in a large frying pan. Pour sauce over the top. Cover and bring to a boil. Reduce heat to low and simmer about 1 hour or until chicken is tender.

Enchiladas

Experiment until you find your own favorite ingredients. Try mixing beans and meat or adding Spicy Chicken (see page 125). Or, for a cheesy enchilada, mix three different cheeses and don't include meat or beans.

What You Need

2 cups Red Chili Sauce (see page 17) or Green Chili Sauce (see page 18)

12 corn tortillas (see Basic Corn Tortillas, page 285)

3 cups shredded beef (see Shredded Beef, page 102) or Refried Beans (see page 211)

2 cups shredded Monterey jack cheese

What You Do

1. Preheat oven to 375°F.

2. Ladle ½ cup Red or Green Chili Sauce into a 9" × 12" baking pan.

3. Put ¼ cup shredded beef or Refried Beans in the center of each tortilla. Add 2 tablespoons shredded cheese. Roll up and place in baking pan.

4. When all the enchiladas are in the baking pan, cover with the remaining sauce and cheese. Bake for 15–20 minutes.

Burritos

Burritos are the "Poor Boy" sandwich of Mexico. They literally contain whatever is leftover from yesterday.

Don't hesitate to add olives, lettuce, or even yesterday's ham.

What You Need

1 cup Refried Beans (see page 211)

1 cup shredded beef (see Shredded Beef, page 102)

1 cup Red Rice (see page 212)

1 (8-ounce) package shredded Cheddar cheese

1 cup tomato salsa (see Tomato Salsa, page 12)

4 flour tortillas (see Flour Tortillas, page 286)

½ cup Red Chili Sauce (see page 17)

½ cup sour cream

½ cup Guacamole (see page 16)

What You Do

1. Heat Refried Beans, Red Rice, and shredded beef on low heat.

2. Add ¼ cup Refried Beans, ¼ cup shredded beef, ¼ cup Red Rice, ¼ cup cheese, and 1 tablespoon tomato salsa to the middle of each tortilla. Drizzle 1 teaspoon of Red Chili Sauce on top. Roll up.

3. Top each burrito with a dollop of sour cream and a dollop of guacamole.

Flautas can be
made with spicy
chicken meat,
ground beef, or
pork.

Beef Flautas

What You Need

16 corn tortillas (see Basic Corn Tortillas, page 285)

3 cups shredded beef (see Shredded Beef, page 102)

1 (6-ounce) package shredded Colby cheese

1 cup vegetable oil

What You Do

1. Place 8 tortillas on a flat surface. Lay 8 more over those, overlapping one about halfway over the other.

2. Spoon about ⅓ cup of shredded beef down the center length, where the tortillas overlap. Sprinkle about 2 tablespoons of cheese on top of the meat. Roll up, starting with one long side and rolling toward the other. Pin closed with wooden picks or small skewers.

3. Heat oil to medium-high in a large frying pan. Fry each flauta until golden brown on both sides.

Serve with
Guacamole (see
page 16), Red Rice
(see page 212), and
Tomato Salsa (see
page 12).

Fajitas

What You Need

1 medium yellow onion

1 green or red bell pepper

1 pound beef (deboned and skinned chicken or
cooked shrimp can be substituted)

1 cup vegetable oil

¼ cup soy sauce

1 teaspoon ground black pepper

¼ teaspoon garlic paste

1 tablespoon Worcestershire sauce

½ tablespoon lemon juice

8 flour tortillas (see Flour Tortillas, page 286)

What You Do

1. Peel onion and cut into 1" pieces. Remove seeds and
   stem from bell pepper and cut into 1" pieces. Cut
   beef and/or chicken into ½" wide strips.

2. Combine vegetable oil, soy sauce, black pepper, garlic, Worcestershire sauce, and lemon juice. Place
   meat in a medium mixing bowl. Pour sauce on top.
   Cover and refrigerate 4–8 hours.

3. Drain meat. Add onion and bell pepper to bowl. Mix
   well. Cook the mixture on medium heat in a large
   frying pan until meat is thoroughly cooked. Serve
   with flour tortillas.

How Do I Marinate Meat?

Never marinate meat for longer than 24 hours. The meat begins to break
down and the texture becomes mushy. The flavors should penetrate
after about 2 hours. Always marinate in the refrigerator so that bacteria
doesn't begin to grow.

Mexican Wedding Cake v

This traditional celebration cake keeps well and actually tastes better after sitting for a day or two.

It's even good without the frosting!

What You Need

2 cups flour

2 teaspoons baking soda

1 20-ounce can crushed pineapple, including juice

1 cup chopped pecans

2 cups granulated sugar

2 eggs

1 (8-ounce) package cream cheese

2 cups powdered sugar

½ cup butter

1 teaspoon vanilla

What You Do

1. Preheat oven to 350°F. Grease and flour a 9" × 13" pan.

2. Combine flour, soda, pineapples with their juice, chopped pecans, granulated sugar, and eggs in a medium mixing bowl. Stir until well mixed. Pour into pan and bake uncovered for 30–35 minutes.

3. For frosting, mix together cream cheese, powdered sugar, butter, and vanilla until well blended. Let cake cool thoroughly before frosting. Sprinkle with more chopped pecans.

Capirotada v

This bread pudding is a Christmas tradition in many Mexican households.

What You Need

8 slices white bread

2 large tart apples

2 cups water

1 cup white sugar

1 cup firmly packed brown sugar

1 teaspoon cinnamon

½ teaspoon nutmeg

½ teaspoon cloves

½ teaspoon salt

2 tablespoons butter

2 cups raisins

2 cups shredded mild Cheddar cheese

What You Do

1. Preheat oven to 350°F.

2. Toast bread and tear into 1" cubes. Peel the apples, remove the cores, and slice the apples into ½" pieces.

3. Combine the water, white sugar, brown sugar, cinnamon, nutmeg, cloves, and salt in a medium saucepan and bring the mixture to a boil. Lower the heat and simmer for 10 minutes until the mixture becomes syrupy.

4. Butter a rectangular baking pan on the bottom and sides. Place the bread cubes on the bottom. Sprinkle the apples and raisins on top. Then sprinkle the cheese on top of that. Pour the syrup over the mixture. Bake in the oven for 30 minutes.

Are Cheese and Fruit Popular in Mexican Menus?

Many Mexican desserts feature milk and fruit products, taking advantage of the two sweetest unprocessed items in their diet. When combined with their wide array of spices, the result is an unusual blending of flavors that at first seems odd but gradually grows to be a pleasant sensation.

Mexican Christmas Salad   v

This is perfect for a buffet dinner because guests can make their own salads, choosing the ingredients they like best.

What You Need

2–6 Key limes

1 cup mayonnaise

3 tablespoons sugar

2 tablespoons whole milk

1 small head iceberg lettuce

3 medium oranges

3 small bananas

2 large sweet apples

2 cups canned sliced beets, drained

1 (20-ounce) can chunk pineapple, drained

½ cup salted, skinless peanuts

What You Do

1. Grate 1 tablespoon of peel from the Key limes. Squeeze ¼ cup juice from the limes. In a bowl, mix the lime juice, lime peel, mayonnaise, sugar, and milk.

2. Slice lettuce into ½" wide strips. Peel oranges and slice thinly. Peel bananas and slice in ¼" rounds. Core apples and cut into ½" thick wedges.

3. Place the bowl of dressing in the middle of a platter and arrange lettuce around it. On the lettuce, arrange separate piles of pineapple, oranges, bananas, apples, and beets. Sprinkle peanuts over the fruit.

What Type of Lettuce Should I Choose?

Different lettuces have very different flavors. Iceberg lettuce tends to be the most mild. Leaf lettuces can be slightly more bitter. Experiment with different types of lettuce or the prepackaged lettuce mixes to find your favorites.

LEVEL **E**

SERVINGS **4**

Serve with Red Rice
(see page 212).

Mayan Lamb

What You Need

2 pounds boneless lamb

½ cup chopped onion

¼ teaspoon garlic paste

1 cup canned diced tomatoes, drained

1 teaspoon salt

¼ teaspoon ground black pepper

1 cup pepitas

1 tablespoon annatto seeds

2 tablespoons vegetable oil

1 tablespoon lemon juice

What You Do

1. Cut lamb into 2" chunks.

2. Put lamb, onion, garlic, tomatoes, salt, and pepper into a heavy saucepot. Stir well. Add water to cover. Bring to a boil, reduce heat, cover, and simmer until meat is tender, about 2 hours.

3. Combine pepitas and annatto seeds in an electric blender or food processor. Blend until pulverized.

4. In a small frying pan, heat oil to medium temperature. Add pepitas and annatto seeds and fry for 2 to 3 minutes, stirring constantly. Stir in lemon juice.

5. Right before serving, stir the seed mixture into the meat sauce.

Mexican Hot Chocolate v

What You Need

1 (3-ounce) package unsweetened chocolate

½ cup white sugar

2 teaspoons cinnamon

1 teaspoon nutmeg

2 cups water

4 cups whole milk

1½ cups whipped cream

What You Do

1. Place chocolate, sugar, cinnamon, nutmeg, and water in large saucepan and heat over low heat until chocolate melts and mixture is smooth.

2. Bring to a boil. Turn heat low and simmer 5 minutes, stirring constantly. Stir in milk. Beat with a hand beater until foamy.

3. Top each cup with a dollop of whipped cream.

Raspberry Atole v

What You Need

½ cup cornmeal

4 cups water

3 cups skim milk

1 cup whipping cream

2 cups fresh raspberries

2 cups white sugar

What You Do

Place the cornmeal, water, milk, and whipping cream in a large saucepan. Heat at medium temperature, stirring constantly. Do not boil. Crush raspberries with a potato masher. When mixture thickens, add the sugar and raspberries as well as the juice from the raspberries. Continue heating, stirring constantly. When mixture produces small bubbles, it is ready to serve.

Mexican Coffee v

What You Need

6 cups water

¼ cup packed brown sugar

1 (3") cinnamon stick

6 whole cloves

¾ cup regular ground, roasted coffee

What You Do

In a medium saucepan, combine water, brown sugar, cinnamon stick, and cloves. Heat at medium temperature, stirring periodically, until sugar is dissolved. Add ground coffee. Bring to a boil, reduce heat, and simmer uncovered for 1 to 2 minutes. Remove from heat. Cover and let stand 15 minutes. Strain before serving.

Chocolate Horchata   v

What You Need

½ cup uncooked white rice

4 cups water

4 cups whole milk

1 (4-ounce) package unsweetened chocolate

2 cups brown sugar

1 teaspoon cayenne pepper

What You Do

1. Grind the rice to a fine powder in a food processor or blender.

2. Place the rice, water, and milk in a large saucepan. Heat at medium temperature, stirring constantly. Do not boil.

3. Grate chocolate with a vegetable grater.

4. When mixture thickens, add the brown sugar, cayenne pepper, and chocolate. Continue heating, stirring constantly. When mixture produces small bubbles, remove from the stove and whip with a hand mixer until it is frothy.

LEVEL **M**

SERVINGS **12**

These traditional treats also can be formed into small patties and served with jam.

Churros v

What You Need

3 cups vegetable oil

1 cup water

½ cup butter

1 cup flour

¼ teaspoon salt

3 eggs

1 cup powdered sugar

¼ cup cinnamon

What You Do

1. Pour oil into a medium frying pan (oil should be 1" to 2" deep). Heat to 375°F. (An electric skillet can be useful here.)

2. Heat water to a rolling boil in medium saucepan. Add butter and continue to boil.

3. Quickly stir in flour and salt. Reduce heat to low and stir vigorously until mixture forms a ball.

4. Remove from heat and beat in eggs one at a time, until the mixture is smooth and glossy.

5. Form dough into 12 round sticks about 10" long and 1" thick.

6. Fry sticks 2 or 3 at a time until light brown.

7. Remove sticks and cool on paper towels.

8. Mix powdered sugar and cinnamon together on a large place. As soon as churros are cool, roll in the mixture. Set aside until completely cool.

What's the Best Way to Fry Food?

Although it seems easy, frying food is a great art. The oil must be hot enough to cook the food without soaking into the food. At the same time, if the oil is too hot, it will cook the outside of the food before the inside is completely cooked.

Pan de Muerto v

This bread is traditionally served on Los Dias de Los Muertos (The Days of the Dead), November 1 and 2, although you can exclude the skull-and-crossbones decoration and make it any time of the year.

What You Need

1 tablespoon (or 1 package) active dry yeast

½ cup warm water

5 eggs

1 tablespoon aniseed

¼ cup butter

½ cup sugar

½ teaspoon salt

½ teaspoon ground nutmeg

2½ cups flour

What You Do

1. Preheat oven to 375°F. Dissolve yeast in ¼ cup warm water. Separate 2 eggs. Beat together 2 eggs plus 2 egg yolks. Steep aniseed in remaining ¼ cup warm water for 10–15 minutes. Melt butter in a small saucepan on low heat.

2. Put the yeast water and 1 tablespoon sugar in a large mixing bowl. Stir gently. Let sit about 10 minutes or until it appears foamy.

3. Stir in salt, ⅓ cup sugar, nutmeg, melted butter, aniseed with water, and the beaten eggs and yolks. Mix well while slowly adding 2½ cups flour. The dough should be slightly sticky. Knead for 10–15 minutes.

4. Lightly coat a large mixing bowl with oil or shortening. Place dough inside and cover with a towel. Place in a warm place and let rise until doubled, usually 1–2 hours.

Pan de Muerto—*continued*

5. Punch the dough down and place it on a floured surface. Remove a handful of dough and set aside. Shape remaining dough into a round loaf about 1" thick and place it on a greased cookie sheet.

6. Make a deep indentation in the center of the loaf with your fist. Form the small piece of dough set aside into 2 "bone" shapes about 4" long and one "skull" shape. Place these in the center indentation.

7. Cover the dough with a towel and place in a warm place to rise for 45 minutes to 1 hour. The dough should hold a fingerprint when pressed.

8. Bake for 30 minutes or until golden brown.

9. Beat remaining egg and use it as a wash on the bread while the bread is still warm. Sprinkle with remaining sugar.

What's Los Dias de Los Muertos?

The Days of the Dead are a holiday time when Mexicans celebrate the return of the souls of their departed loved ones. It is a time of celebration with memorial altars set up for the dead souls who will, according to the tradition, be streaming through tears in the veil between the worlds to visit their families and have a brief taste of living once again. Their favorite foods and trinkets will decorate the altars, and families pack up baskets of holiday foods, candles, flowers, and tequila to picnic at the gravesides of their loved ones. Though it may sound somber to those from other traditions, this is actually a very festive, happy holiday.

Turn the loaf onto a platter then sprinkle the top with brown sugar.

Place it under the broiler and lightly brown the top immediately before serving.

Traditional Flan v

What You Need

8 eggs

⅔ cup white sugar

¼ teaspoon salt

3½ cups evaporated milk

2 teaspoons vanilla extract

½ cup light brown sugar

What You Do

1. Preheat oven to 350°F.

2. In a medium mixing bowl, beat eggs until yolks and whites are well blended. Add white sugar and salt. Beat in evaporated milk and vanilla extract.

3. Sprinkle brown sugar onto the bottom of a loaf pan. Gently pour the custard mixture over the brown sugar.

4. Place the loaf pan in a shallow baking pan containing hot water. Place in oven. Bake for 1 hour or until a knife inserted into the center comes out clean.

5. Refrigerate 8–12 hours before serving.

What are the Different Kinds of Sugar?

Brown sugar is actually white sugar with molasses added. White sugar usually comes from either beets or sugar cane. Cane sugar actually tastes slightly sweeter. Confectioners' sugar is finely ground white sugar.

Serve with Mexican Coleslaw (see page 93).

Beef Tamales

What You Need

48 large, dry corn husks

½ cup lard

2 cups masa harina

2 cups chicken stock (see Chicken Stock, page 124)

2 cups shredded beef (see Shredded Beef, page 102)

What You Do

1. Wash corn husks in warm water. Put in a saucepan and cover with boiling water. Let soak at least 30 minutes before using.

2. Beat lard until light and fluffy. Gradually beat in masa harina and chicken stock until dough sticks together and has a paste-like consistency.

3. Shake excess water from each softened corn husk and pat dry on paper towels. Overlap 2 husks half-way side-by-side. Spread about 2 tablespoons of dough on center portion of doubled husk. Spoon about 1½ tablespoons shredded beef onto the dough. Wrap tamale, overlapping sides and then folding up top and bottom.

4. Lay tamales on top of extra dozen corn husks in the top section of a steamer with the open flaps on the bottom. Steam over simmering water about 1 hour or until corn husk can be easily peeled from dough.

How Do I Use a Double Boiler?

A double boiler consists of two pots, one sitting on top of the other. The food to be cooked goes in the top pot while boiling water is in the bottom. The steam from the boiling water cooks the food. By not having direct contact with the heat source, you eliminate the possibility of burning the food, while still being able to get it very hot.

These are just as good cold as they are hot.

Many Mexican children and blue collar workers carry these for their lunches.

Empanaditas de Carne

What You Need

1 pound beef roast

1 pound pork roast

3 cups flour

1 teaspoon baking powder

2 teaspoons salt

1 cup plus 1 tablespoon sugar

3 tablespoons shortening

1 egg

1 cup water

1 cup raisins

2 cups applesauce

1 teaspoon ground cinnamon

½ teaspoon crushed cloves

½ cup chopped pecans

4 cups vegetable oil

What You Do

1. Put beef roast and pork roast in a pot and add water just to cover meat. Cover pot and turn heat to medium. Simmer until meat is completely cooked, at least 1 hour.

2. Combine flour, baking powder, 1 teaspoon salt, and 1 tablespoon sugar. Blend in shortening.

3. Beat egg in a separate bowl and slowly add to flour mixture. Add water. Roll dough to about ⅛" thick and cut with a biscuit cutter.

4. Remove meat from bones. Discard bones and grind meat with a meat grinder or food processor. Place meat in a large pot. Add raisins, applesauce, remaining 1 cup sugar, cinnamon, cloves, remaining 1 teaspoon salt, and ½ cup chopped pecans. Add enough meat stock to thoroughly moisten.

5. Simmer uncovered for 15 minutes, adding more water if mixture seems dry. Make sure the mixture holds together, though. It should not be runny.

6. Put about 3 tablespoons of meat mixture in the center of each of the biscuits. Fold over and pinch edges shut.

7. Heat oil in a large frying pan until medium hot. Add several empanaditas. Fry on both sides until golden brown. Place on paper towels to cool.

Chili Rellenos

Serve as an appetizer or a vegetable dish to accompany any meat or bean dish.

What You Need

6 large poblano peppers

1 (8-ounce) block mozzarella cheese

1 small white onion

½ tablespoon olive oil

¼ cup canned chopped jalapeño peppers, drained

2 cups canned diced tomatoes with juice

2 cups chicken stock (see Chicken Stock, page 124)

2 tablespoons corn starch

3 eggs

2 cups cornmeal

1 teaspoon salt

What You Do

1. Preheat oven to 350°F. Put poblano peppers in the preheated oven. Turn when the tops are white. When both sides are white, remove peppers and let cool. Peel skin from peppers. Cut cheese in wedges about ½" wide. Stuff wedges into the peppers.

2. Peel onion and chop into ¼" pieces. In a medium saucepan, heat olive oil to medium temperature. Add onions. Cook until onions are brown. Add chopped jalapeño peppers and tomatoes with their juice. Add chicken stock. Add corn starch. Cook on medium heat, stirring constantly, until sauce is the consistency of gravy.

3. Beat eggs then combine with cornmeal. Mix well. If the mixture is not sticky, add water until it is about the consistency of thick pancake batter.

4. Dip poblano peppers into egg and cornmeal batter and put peppers into a lightly greased frying pan on medium heat. Cook until brown on one side then flip and cook until brown on all sides.

5. Cover with sauce before serving.

This recipe yields 2 quarts.

Although you might be tempted to strain this drink before serving, the solid ingredients actually are eaten as a sort of wet salad after the drink is gone.

Candlemas Drink   v

What You Need

1 pound canned beets

½ cup pitted prunes

1 cup head lettuce

1 green apple

¼ cup blanched almonds

1½ quarts water

½ cup sugar

¼ cup seedless raisins

¼ cup unsalted peanuts

What You Do

1. Chop beets into ¼" pieces. Chop prunes into ¼" pieces. Shred lettuce. Peel and remove core from apple and chop into ¼" pieces. Chop almonds into small pieces.

2. Pour water into a glass or ceramic container. Dissolve sugar in water. Add all ingredients. Stir gently. Refrigerate 3–4 hours before serving.

Rabbit from Oaxaca

Serve with Extra
Special Frijoles
Refritos (see page
221).

What You Need

2 medium zucchini

4 medium baking potatoes

4 medium carrots

1 large yellow onion

2 medium red tomatoes

¼ cup canned jalapeño peppers, drained

2 tablespoons butter

1 cut-up rabbit (3–5 pounds)

1 cup dry white wine

1 cup chicken stock (see Chicken Stock, page 124)

What You Do

1. Preheat oven to 350°F. Remove stems from zucchini and quarter. Peel potatoes and quarter. Peel carrots and quarter. Peel onion and quarter. Remove stems from tomatoes and quarter. Drain juice from jalapeño peppers.

2. Melt butter in a large frying pan on medium heat. Add rabbit pieces and fry until lightly browned on all sides. Put rabbit pieces in an ovenproof casserole.

3. Arrange zucchini, potatoes, carrots, onion, jalapeño peppers, and tomatoes around and on top of rabbit pieces

4. Mix white wine and chicken stock. Pour over the top of the rabbit and vegetables. Bake in oven for 1½ hours.

Serve this as a bedtime treat or dessert drink.

Nonalcoholic Rampope v

What You Need

4 cups whole milk

½ cup sugar

12 egg yolks

¼ cup skinless sliced almonds

1 teaspoon cinnamon

1 teaspoon vanilla extract

2 tablespoons rum flavoring

What You Do

1. Put the milk and sugar into a medium-sized pan on the stove and heat at medium-high temperature until it reaches a boil. Reduce heat and simmer for 10 minutes, stirring constantly. Remove from heat and cool to room temperature.

2. Separate the eggs and discard the whites. Beat the yolks with a fork until they are thick and frothy.

3. Add the yolks slowly to the milk and sugar mixture. Beat the mixture gently until the yolks are integrated into the milk and sugar. Add the sliced almonds, vanilla extract, rum flavoring, and cinnamon.

4. Put the mixture back on the stove and cook on medium heat, stirring constantly, until the mixture thickens enough to coat a spoon.

5. Store in a covered glass container in the refrigerator for at least 48 hours before serving.

Kings' Bread Ring v

What You Need

3 eggs

2 teaspoons (or 2 packages) active dry yeast

½ cup warm water

½ cup milk

⅓ cup sugar

⅓ cup shortening

2 teaspoons salt

4 cups all purpose flour

2 cups chopped candied fruits: citron, cherries, orange peel

tiny china doll (approximately 1" high)

½ cup melted butter

1⅓ cups confectioners' sugar

4 teaspoons water

½ teaspoon vanilla extract

What You Do

1. Preheat oven to 375°F.

2. Beat eggs until blended. Dissolve yeast in water. Heat milk in a saucepan at medium-high temperature until scalded. Put regular sugar, shortening, and salt in a bowl. Pour in scalded milk and mix until sugar is dissolved and shortening is melted. Cool to lukewarm. Beat in 1 cup flour, eggs, and yeast. Add more flour to make a stiff dough. Stir in 1½ cups candied fruits.

3. Turn dough onto a floured surface and knead until smooth. Roll dough under hands into a long rope; shape into a ring, sealing ends together. Transfer to a greased cookie sheet. Push the tiny china doll into dough so it is covered. Melt butter in a small saucepan over low heat. Brush the ring with butter.

4. Cover with a towel and let rise in a warm place until it doubles in size, about 1½ hours. Bake 25–30 minutes or until golden brown. Cool on a wire rack.

5. Blend 1⅓ cups confectioners' sugar, 4 teaspoons water, and ½ teaspoon vanilla extract to make an icing. When bread is cool, spread icing over the top.

Serve with Spinach Salad (see page 89).

Polenta v

What You Need

4½ cups cold water

1½ cups yellow cornmeal

1 small yellow onion

1 garlic clove

1 tablespoon olive oil

2 pounds canned diced tomatoes, drained

1 bay leaf

½ teaspoon dried basil

1 teaspoon salt

½ teaspoon black pepper

1 teaspoon white sugar

1 (8-ounce) package shredded fontina cheese

1 (8-ounce) package shredded Gorgonzola cheese

1 bunch fresh parsley

What You Do

1. Preheat oven to 400°F.

2. Put cold water into a saucepan on medium-high. Add cornmeal. Whisk cornmeal into the cold water. Continue whisking while bringing to a boil. Cook 15 minutes, stirring frequently. Pour into a 9" × 12" pan. Let sit. Cut into 3" × 3" squares and remove from pan.

3. Peel onion and garlic and chop finely. In a large frying pan, add olive oil and heat to medium. Cook onion and garlic for 3–5 minutes or until onion is limp and clear. Set aside.

4. Put tomatoes, bay leaf, basil, salt, pepper, and sugar in a saucepan on medium heat. Bring to a boil. Reduce heat to low and simmer for 15 minutes. Add onion and garlic to tomato mixture. Mash with a potato masher or blend in a food processor or blender.

5. Spread 1 cup sauce in the bottom of the 9" × 12" pan. Lean squares at an angle in the pan. Between each square, add about ½ cup of grated cheeses. Pour remaining sauce over the polenta and cheese squares. Bake for 25–35 minutes. Garnish with parsley.

Serve as a breakfast treat with Easy Huevos Rancheros (see page 129).

Molletes ᵥ

What You Need

4 eggs

½ cup warm water

½ cup butter

2 teaspoons (or 2 packages) active dry yeast

½ cup sugar

½ teaspoon salt

1 tablespoon aniseed

4½ cups all purpose flour

2 tablespoons light corn syrup

What You Do

1. Preheat oven to 350°F.

2. Leave eggs out until room temperature. Add warm water to a bowl and sprinkle yeast on top. Stir until it dissolves. Melt butter in a small pan on low heat.

3. Add sugar, salt, aniseed, melted butter, 3 eggs, and 2 cups of flour to bowl. Beat until smooth. Stir in enough additional flour to make a soft dough.

4. Turn dough onto a lightly floured surface; knead until smooth and elastic (about 10 minutes). Put dough into a greased bowl; turn to grease top. Cover and let rise in a warm place until double its size, about 1 hour.

6. Punch dough down and turn onto a lightly floured surface. Roll into a 12" square. Cut into quarters and cut each square into 4 triangles. Place triangles on a greased cookie sheet, allowing space for rising. Cover and let rise in a warm place until double their size, about 1 hour.

8. Separate yolk and white from remaining egg. Discard white. Beat egg yolk and corn syrup together until well blended. Generously brush over triangles.

9. Bake 10 to 15 minutes or until lightly browned. Serve warm.

Appendix A

Meals

ﾟᐟ

Brunch

Holiday Meal and Treats

Celebration Meal

Appendix B
Glossary of Mexican Food and Cooking Terms

achiote: a seasoning paste made from the seed of the annatto tree

adobado or adobo: mexican barbecue sauce

agua fresca: literally "fresh water"; refers to nonalcoholic teas and juices

ajo: garlic

ancho: a dried poblano pepper

añejo: aged, as in cheese or liquor

arroz: rice

asada: roasted or grilled

blanco: white

brazo de reina: literally "queen's arm"; a type of large tamale

cajeta: caramel

caldo: broth

canela: cinnamon

carne: meat, usually beef

carnitas: meat chunks

cascabel: a small, red dried chili pepper

ceviche: a dish of small fish pieces marinated in lime juice

chayote: a small, green squash

chilaca: a long, thin, dark brown chili pepper

chili negro: a dried chilaca pepper

chipotle: a smoked and dried jalapeño pepper

comal: a round, flat earthenware griddle (used for cooking tortillas)

comino: cumin

crema: Mexican sour cream

enchilada: stuffed and rolled tortillas with chili sauce

enfrijolada: stuffed and rolled tortillas in bean sauce

enmolada: stuffed and rolled tortillas in mole sauce

epazote: a wild herb used as a seasoning

escabèche: a sweet and sour marinade

fresca: fresh

frijoles: beans

frijoles refritos: Refried Beans

fuerte: a type of avocado

habanero: a type of chili pepper

huevos: eggs

jalapeño: a type of chili pepper

jicama: a white root vegetable usually eaten raw

lima: lime

limón: lemon

maiz: corn

manzanilla: a small green olive

masa: corn dough

mesa: table

molcajete y tejolete: a mortar and pestle; used to grind spices

mole: a traditional sauce made with a variation of spices, nuts, chili peppers, and Mexican chocolate

morita: a small dried chili

naranja agria: a type of orange from the Yucatan

nopale: cactus paddle

nopalitos: "baby" cactus paddles

pasilla: a dried chilaca chili pepper

pepita: pumpkin seed

pescado: fish

picadillo: ground meat seasoned with spices, nuts, peppers, and sometimes fruit

picholines: large green olives

pico de gallo: a salsa made of fresh tomatoes

placa: a round, flat cast-iron griddle (used for cooking and warming tortillas)

poblano: a type of green chili pepper

pollo: chicken

pozole: a traditional stew with meat and hominy

raja: a roasted chili pepper strip

ranchero: ranch or country-style

salsa: sauce or dip

sandía: watermelon

seca: dry

serrano: a small, green chili

sopa: soup

tomatillo: a small green fruit that looks like a tomato

torta: sandwich

verde: green

Index of Cooking Questions

Index